Local 34

won representation, and ultimately a contract, through fresh demands, democratic methods, innovative tactics, mass pressure, and broad alliances—the very ingredients which have characterized the more dynamic labor struggles of the American past. . . . The themes of dignity and social justice, the process of rank-and-file engagement and initiative, the instinct for daring and experimentation, the reliance on broad alliances and popular pressure, are all woven through the heritage of American working people; they link the Knights of Labor of the 1880s to the Congress of Industrial Organizations of the 1930s, the Industrial Workers of the World of the early twentieth century to the United Farm Workers of recent times, the Populists of the 1890s to the Civil Rights Movement of the 1950s and 1960s. These qualities are essential to the prospects for a resurgence of the American labor movement today.

—from the Introduction

Solidarity

It is we who push the papers, put the paychecks
   in the mail;
It is we who type the letters, mind the office
   without fail.
And until we get a contract, it is we who'll
   shut down Yale,
For the union makes us strong.

Solidarity forever, etc.

Your experiments depend on us, we tally up
   the stats;
We work with agar-agar, pour the chemicals in vats.
But until we get a contract, we won't feed
   your stupid rats,
And the union makes us strong.

Solidarity forever, etc.

It is Bart who hires the lawyers, it is Bart
   who calls the shots;
He treats his women workers like a bunch of
   timid tots.
It is Bartlett who has tied the university in knots,
But the union makes us strong.

Solidarity forever, etc.

We are coming out to picket, we are marching
   out en masse;
If you can't see fit to join us, it will only be your loss.
It's the workers who are standing for Lux et Veritas,
And the union makes us strong.

Solidarity forever, etc.

The Yale strikers wrote their own versions of many labor and
popular songs, and produced their own song book.

On Strike for Respect

The Clerical and Technical Workers' Strike at Yale University, 1984–85

Toni Gilpin, Gary Isaac, Dan Letwin,
and Jack McKivigan

Foreword by David Montgomery

University of Illinois Press
Urbana and Chicago

This book is printed on acid-free paper.

Library of Congress Cataloging-in-Publication Data

On strike for respect : the clerical and technical workers' strike at
    Yale University, 1984–85 / Toni Gilpin . . . [et al.] ; foreword by
    David Montgomery.
        p.   cm.
    Originally published: Chicago : C. H. Kerr, 1988.
    ISBN 978-0-252-06454-8 (paper : acid-free paper)
    1. Yale University—Employees. 2. Strikes and lockouts—
Connecticut. 3. Federation of University Employees. I. Gilpin,
Toni.
LD6309.05   1995
378.746'8—dc20   94-22669
                                                           CIP

Foreword

How can working people win today? What should they try to win? The story of the unionization and strike of clerical and technical employees at Yale University helps us answer both those questions.

Since the mid-1970s the American labor movement has been battered by plant closings, company demands for concessions, systematic destruction of industry-wide agreements and of pattern bargaining, renegotiation of signed contracts under threats of bankruptcy, and reorganization of international trade by multinational corporations, whose speculative designs show no interest whatever in the welfare of American workers and communities. Real earnings ceased to grow, and middle-income jobs became increasingly scarce, so that each passing year has seen inequalities of income become more glaring. After 1980 the assault was intensified, as the government dismantled regulatory agencies that had formerly provided some security for workers' health and for the union standards, revamped the National Labor Relations Board and the Civil Rights Commission to strengthen employers' hands, and ruthlessly smashed the air traffic controllers' union as a signal to the whole country that a new era had arrived. Every day in every way the government and the media celebrate these developments as a triumph of individualism, of the unfettered market, and of new prosperity for the fortunate few.

The clerical and technical employees at Yale challenged this new era head-on. They did so by breathing new life into the beleaguered labor movement. They joined a major AFL-CIO union, filed for and won an NLRB certification election, went on strike, and successfully negotiated a first contract. All those things had been accomplished by other workers many times before. They represent the established practice of modern unionism in the United States. What was new in the Yale struggle was the workers' sense of organization, their goal of equality, and their spirit of solidarity. All three were rooted in the daily lives of the people involved, and all three represented a repudiation of Reaganite ideology.

Organization came first. The hundreds of activists who made Local 34 tick knew that a union is organized not once, but every day. The need of the hour was not simply to sign people up, but to make them active members of elaborate networks of action and discussion that reached into every corner of the enterprise. The endless round of lunchtime gatherings, the consultations between negotiating committee members and their departmental constituents, and the lively debates on picket lines were what allowed two thousand women and men to decide what they wanted and how they were going to get it. Organization overcame the isolation and helplessness of individuals. The demands arose out of the organization.

The union's demands stressed equality: standard rates for clearly defined tasks, equal pay for jobs of comparable worth, and ladders of progression that all employees could ascend together. The money demands were designed to end the systematic underpayment of jobs filled mainly by women, to rebuild that threatened middle-income group of earners, and to make a respectable retirement possible. Invigorating all these demands was the battle-cry of "respect." Women and men, white, black, Hispanic, and Asian employees together sought treatment and earnings that reflected their contributions to the University.

Their goals were won through solidarity. First and foremost came the daily manifestations of unity in their own ranks and the unstinting support offered the clerical and technical employees by Yale's service and maintenance workers. Sharing strike benefits with each other, walking the lines day after day, mobilizing large and enthusiastic demonstrations, and going to jail together, the strikers infused the University with a mood of mutual concern and support. They reached out to New Haven residents, to students, and to other employees of the University, involving all of them in strike activities.

After the end of the strike the victorious members of Local 34 charted a three-point plan of action for the future: to build the union continuously in every department, to make New Haven a union town, and to ally themselves with black workers in South Africa and the campaign for divestment of Yale's funds from that country.

The U.S. labor movement has been beaten down and revived again many times during the last 150 years. Its revivals have always been animated by a sense of organization, equality, and solidarity similar in some ways to the one recounted in this book. Today, however, those principles have assumed added meaning. They are indispensable to union success in this grim epoch. Beyond that, they also provide the keys to a necessary redefinition of labor's goals. Only when working people are organized into unions they control can they even decide what they want. Only through solidarity can they hope to win it. Many similar struggles throughout the land will be required if American working men and women are to chart a path toward a community life based on their needs and welfare. As the members of Local 34 learned early in their battle: no union, no matter how large, militant, and resourceful, is big enough to stand alone.

David Montgomery

Acknowledgments

This book describes the making of a union of clerical and technical workers at Yale University and that union's 1984-85 strike. The study grew out of our participation in student and faculty support activities for the union's organizing campaign and strike. However, we should stress that despite cooperation from members of Local 34, this is not an "official" history of the campaign. Nor does this book seek to offer the exhaustive treatment that the story of Local 34 deserves, and will someday receive. Our purpose, rather, has been to tell the story of Local 34 while it remained fresh and of immediate relevance.

We would like to thank William Cronon, Mary Grimes, and Tom Keenan for furnishing us with documents from the campaign and strike, and Michael Mandler for his contributions to our understanding of the economic aspects of the union's negotiations and contract.

—The Authors

Introduction

Management seldom welcomes a union into the workplace with open arms, and whenever workers organize to have one anyway, it is an act of self-assertion charged with drama. However, not long after the Federation of University Employees, an affiliate of the Hotel and Restaurant Employees International Union (HERE), launched a campaign to build Local 34, a union of clerical and technical workers at Yale University, it became clear that a drama of a remarkable sort was unfolding. One had only to look at the workers involved—the vast majority women, most of them secretaries, librarians, and laboratory technicians—to see that these were not the typical recruits of organized labor. Moreover, in Yale University, these workers were up against a formidable adversary. Wealthy, paternalistic, and distinctly unreceptive to the idea that a union should "come between" the administration and its white collar workers, Yale could not be challenged without deep reserves of creativity and resilience.

There are broader meanings to the story of Local 34 as well. The 1980s have taken a heavy toll on progressive movements in America, and for working people the impact has been especially pronounced. The labor movement has been hurt by a shrinking industrial base, a hostile federal administration, a growing public indifference to unions, and union bureaucracies that are short on innovation and resistant to rank-and-file participation. Under these circumstances, labor has suffered its greatest setbacks in half a century: stalled organizing drives, failed strikes, concessions bargaining, and union decertifications. The women's movement has similarly suffered under attack from the Right while racism, institutional and otherwise, has gathered renewed strength.   It is in this sobering context that the story of Local 34 draws its deepest significance. At a time when long-established unions are struggling to survive, here is a previously unorganized work unit battling successfully for representation. At a time when strikes are becoming less and less frequent and more and more defensive, here is a group of workers who achieve substantial gains through a hard-fought strike. And in a labor movement which has generally been the domain of blue collar men, here is a union whose membership is mostly female, disproportionately minority, and by and large inexperienced in unions, let alone strikes. It is our purpose in this book to explore what it was about the Yale organizing campaign that helped to bring about these unusual outcomes.

The range of issues the union raised reflected a membership which, perhaps partly because of its general inexperience in trade union matters, brought a tremendous creativity and sense of possibility to the struggle. In addition to such traditional issues as union recognition, wages, and job security, Local 34 went on to demand that the University administration acknowledge and rectify the concentration of women and minorities at the lower end of Yale's job scale; thus comparable worth, although never a formal demand, became a principal rallying cry for the union and its supporters. Another distinctive issue concerned the place of white collar employees in an academic community. Yale workers who had long felt unappreciated ("invisible" was the word often used) were asserting their claim to the respect which they felt their contributions to the University had earned them.

Another meaningful layer of the story was the democratic character of the union. The structure of the Local and the attitudes of its staff and members fostered a degree of rank-and-file involvement all too rare in the modern American labor movement. This grassroots approach gave members a sense that the union was truly their own.

Local 34's campaign also deserves attention for the variety of tactics that it developed. Faced with the challenge of overcoming a powerful employer in an uncommon setting, the union developed an instinct for unusual, even startling turns of strategy that would more than once rescue the campaign from an unpromising situation. However, more than sheer inventiveness distinguished Local 34's tactics. Throughout the organizing drive and the strike, the union stressed the vital importance of public pressure in bringing the Yale administration around; what happened inside the bargaining room, leaders often asserted, was a direct reflection of what was happening outside. This attitude provided a refreshing departure from the widespread "business union" philosophy, according to which labor disputes are best left to the professional negotiators and the lawyers.

Following from this strategy was a sustained effort to keep the controversy in the public eye. The union found early on that, although the University lacked one of the soft spots that other industries face in labor conflicts—lost sales—it was extraordinarily sensitive to negative publicity. Thus, throughout the campaign, day-to-day organizing would be punctuated with "events," such as rallies, petition drives, and "town meetings," designed to draw media attention to the strike. And there was more to these practices than embarrassing Yale. They also provided ways for Local 34 members to articulate their battle as a social cause of historic importance. This emphasis, set against Yale's failure to abide by its enlightened ideals, gave the union a moral luster that would sustain members and supporters during difficult times.

Finally, Local 34 cultivated a broad network of support, both local and national. The most crucial source of support was the maintenance and service work force of Yale, already organized as Local 35 of the Federation of University Employees. Their willingness to honor the picket lines of the clerical and technical workers through a ten-week strike provided a rare example of sustained solidarity between blue and white collar workers, without which it is unlikely Local 34 could have succeeded. In addition, the union received impressive measures of backing from other quarters, ranging from students and faculty at Yale, to public figures and groups from all parts of the New Haven community, to labor, women's, and civil rights organizations from around the country.

In sum, Local 34 won representation, and ultimately a contract, through fresh demands, democratic methods, innovative tactics, mass pressure, and broad alliances—the very ingredients which have characterized the more dynamic labor struggles of the American past.

Indeed, the very feeling of inventiveness that galvanized the campaign revealed how much from past experience has been lost to the American labor movement. The themes of dignity and social justice, the process of rank-and-file engagement and initiative, the instinct for daring and experimentation, the reliance on broad alliances and popular pressure, are all woven through the heritage of American working people; they link the Knights of Labor of the 1880s to the Congress of Industrial Organizations of the 1930s, the Industrial Workers of the World of the early twentieth century to the United Farm Workers of recent times, the Populists of the 1890s to the Civil Rights Movement of the 1950s and 1960s. These qualities are essential to the prospects for a resurgence of the American labor movement today.

Beneath the Ivy:
Work and Power at Yale

I n Yale University's main library there is a special shelf
set aside for the novels and short stories that celebrate the
Yale tradition. Here one can find *Boltwood at Yale* and Walter
Camp's *Danny the Freshman*, *Football Days* and *The Big Year*.
Perhaps the most well-known among these books is Owen Johnson's
Stover at Yale, written in 1911.

In the novel's opening chapter, freshman Dink Stover arrives in
New Haven, Connecticut and catches his first awestruck glimpse of
Yale University:

Behind him remained the city, suddenly hushed. He was on the cam-
pus, the Brick Row at his left, in the distance the crowded line
of the fence, the fence where he later should sit in joyful conclave.
Somewhere there in the great protecting embrace of these walls were
the friends that should be his, that should pass with him through
those wonderful years of happiness and good fellowship that were
coming.

"And this is it—this is Yale," he said reverently, with a little tight-
ening of the breath.

This is the Yale that many know. Prestigious and powerful, Yale
has long been a training ground for the nation's elite. The massive
ivy-covered gothic buildings that dominate the campus serve as sym-
bols of the institution's importance. Since 1789, Yale men have held
some 10% of the United States' major diplomatic posts; fifteen
members of Congress each year, on average, are Yale graduates. President and Supreme Court Chief Justice William Howard Taft went

to Yale, as did John C. Calhoun. William F. Buckley and George Bush are Yalies also. Students at Yale, now as in the past, take classes with some of the nation's most famous professors, and can make use of the school's huge library system and significant art collections. Visitors to the campus can peer into Mory's, the private eating club, or look at the strange, windowless buildings that house the "secret societies"—Yale's low-profile answer to fraternities. And thousands of alumni, bedecked in Yale blue, pour into New Haven every other year to revel in grand tradition and urge the Bulldogs to victory as the campus hosts the Yale-Harvard football game.

Yale's image embraces other things as well. For some time, the University has cultivated an enlightened and liberal reputation. Yale, like many colleges and universities, is presented as a haven for the free exchange of opinion; Yale's venerable motto—"*Lux et Veritas*" ("Light and Truth")—reflects the University's oft-proclaimed commitment to unfettered scholarly pursuit. Recently Yale has drawn national attention for more specific "liberal" activities. The University's president during the strike, A. Bartlett Giamatti, had frequently taken progressive stands on public issues. Giamatti criticized Jerry Falwell and the Moral Majority and promised that the University would make up the difference if any of its students failed to get federal loans because they refused to register for the draft.

But beneath its liberal veneer, Yale remains an institution of and for the privileged. Some of the indicators of this are obvious, for instance the $16,000 charged undergraduates for tuition, room and board each year. In other respects Yale's character is less readily apparent. It would take some observation to note that only 5% of Yale's permanent tenured faculty positions, for example, are held by women. One would have to learn some Yale history to discover that the University did not admit women into its undergraduate college until 1969, and that for a time after this, there were still areas of the campus that remained "off limits" to women, including the library's most comfortable reading room, which with its overstuffed green chairs and massive fireplace, suggests a hunt club more than a study area.

Yale's elite position is all the more striking when contrasted to the city surrounding it. Most visitors to the campus are unaware that the 1980 United States census showed New Haven to be the seventh poorest city in the nation. It is easy to remain oblivious to New Haven's poverty while at Yale; the campus is insular and clearly separate from its surroundings. Most students seldom stray far from the campus area. Few of the city's residents, the majority of whom are black or Hispanic, mingle with Yale students; they do not browse through the library or take in University films. Although the University makes use of New Haven services such as fire and police protection, it pays virtually no taxes to the city. Despite the efforts of many citizens' groups over the years to "make Yale pay," the University has successfully resisted any change in its tax-exempt status, claiming that the value of the services which Yale provides to the community compensates for its failure to contribute directly to the city treasury. However, it is doubtful that Yale really wants to attract many of New Haven's poor residents to its grounds. When University officials speak of the "Yale community," New Haven's residents—particularly those from the poorer sections—are not meant to be included.

Yale's "community," so often extolled by President Giamatti, neglects some other important people as well. The University's clerical and technical workers (C&Ts) are seldom featured in Yale's literature or its glossy promotions; they are given no place in the frequent references to "the students, faculty, and administrators" that make up the University. They have not been overlooked because their work is unimportant. On the contrary, the 2,650 clerical and technical workers at Yale keep the University functioning on a daily basis. Their contributions are crucial to the operations of all three campus "areas": the medical school, the central area (where most administrative offices, dormitories, and the humanities departments are located), and Science Hill.

The term "clerical and technical" covers a wide variety of campus workers. Some are secretaries; others are administrative assistants, telephone operators, computer programmers, or athletic trainers. Still others work in the University's libraries as cataloguers and shelvers, in its laboratories as research and development technicians, animal technicians, and autopsy technicians, and in Yale's hospital and health centers as licensed practical nurses and psychiatric aides. Approximately 82% are female, and 14% black. Some fit the old stereotypes of the University secretary—faculty wives, whose salary supplements already comfortable family earnings. Many more are single heads of households or second wage-earners whose paychecks are crucial to their family's income.

Yale has not traditionally treated its clerical and technical work force in a particularly enlightened or generous manner. Before they won a union contract in 1985, full-time C&Ts at Yale earned an average of $13,424 a year. (The United States Bureau of Labor Statistics determined in 1981 that a New England family of four needed at least $16,402 annually to maintain a *low* standard of living.) While Yale is New Haven's largest employer, its salaries for C&Ts lagged well behind those of the city's second largest employer, the Southern New England Telephone Company. Nor could C&Ts look forward to a comfortable retirement after they ended their Yale careers. For retirees who had put in an average of over 18 years at Yale, pensions in 1983 averaged only $171 a month.

As low as these figures were, there were issues that frustrated many of Yale's clerical and technical workers even more. It was difficult, for instance, for C&Ts to increase their incomes significantly, for achieving the maximum within one of Yale's eleven C&T salary grades was a rarity. Although the average C&T in 1983 had put in six years at the University, less than 3% were earning the maximum salary.

Before Local 34 began to organize, few C&Ts had such statistics at their disposal but most grew aware over time that they could not go far in their jobs at Yale. The lack of formal mechanisms for promotions and transfers sharpened resentments. When a Yale employee applied for a promotion or transfer to another office or laboratory there was no requirement that management take skill, experience, or years on the job under consideration. The absence of such fixed guidelines enabled supervisory personnel to distribute jobs and raises to whomever they wished, often to family members, personal friends, or office sycophants.

Many of Yale's C&Ts came to believe that these conditions reflected a basic lack of respect for their contributions to the University. From the outset, Local 34 made the battle for "respect"—rather than a specific call for higher salaries or better pensions—the central thrust of its organizing effort. Many C&Ts who joined the union came to see their fight at Yale as part of the national struggle to recognize the value of "women's work." In fact, the union argued that pay inequity at Yale was even greater than it was nationally. Local 34 gathered statistics revealing that women C&Ts at Yale earned less than their male counterparts—even though the women averaged more years of service. Yale's black employees earned less than their white colleagues, although black workers had on average been employed longer at the University. Thus when Local 34 members went on strike for "respect" in 1984, they called on Yale to redress the systematic manner in which the University undervalued the work performed by the clerical and technical employees. As much as any lawsuit, the walkout at Yale concerned the issue of "comparable worth."

Throughout the union's organizing drive and strike, University administrators maintained that the University could not afford substantial pay and benefit increases for its clerical and technical employees. This argument was not based on sheer lack of capital; Yale's endowment—the sum total of the University's wealth—amounts to over $1.1 billion. In 1983, the University posted a $35 million surplus over operating expenses, which, by its own accounting rules, it plowed back into the endowment. President Giamatti thus declared the budget "balanced," and argued that there was no extra cash available to increase C&Ts' salaries. In fact, as the union pointed out, to meet the C&Ts' demands, the University would simply have had to direct a portion of the $35 million surplus to its clerical workers.

The issue was not whether Yale had the money—it was a question of priorities. Yale's vice-president for administration, Bruce Chrisman, declared that equal pay for equal work "is something all of society is wrestling with. Yale prides itself in being a leader in the community. But it's not always possible for a given institution to be a leader on all fronts." In light of the power structure at Yale, the abrogation of this kind of leadership role was not surprising;

despite the presence of a few prominent liberals, the Yale Corporation has always been dominated by eminently successful businessmen. Of the 17 Corporation members at the time of the strike, three were widely regarded as the most influential in shaping Yale's financial decisions: J. Richardson Dilworth, financial advisor to the Rockefeller family; John B. Madden, managing partner in the Brown Brothers Harriman & Co. Bank; and Cyrus Vance, former Secretary of State and current member of the boards of U.S. Steel, Manufacturers Hanover Trust, IBM, and the *New York Times*. It was unlikely that men such as these would determine that comparable worth—or clerical unionism—were appropriate areas in which Yale should stake out a position of leadership.

Students and faculty members—and of course Yale workers and New Haven citizens—are excluded from any ability to affect the makeup of Yale's board of trustees. Indeed, even alumni elect just six of its members. Nor does Yale have any of the institutions which might attempt to shape Corporation policy: the University lacks any kind of faculty senate and the undergraduates have no college council or student government. "Democracy" is a relative concept at Yale.

The Yale Corporation has not been used to taking directions from or even listening to "outsiders." It was therefore not surprising that the University would resist so strongly the efforts by its clerical and technical workers to organize. Nor was it unusual that once Local 34 won certification, the University attempted to dictate, rather than negotiate, the terms of the union's first contract.

Organizing for Respect

The drive that culminated in the election of Local 34 as the union of clerical and technical employees at Yale was by no means the first effort to organize workers at the University. The service and maintenance employees at the University had been organized in one form or another since the late 1930s, and the existence of the blue collar union on campus had long encouraged Yale's clerical and technical employees to attempt to form their own union.

The first attempt was made in the early 1950s by the Distributive, Processing, and Office Workers' Union. Over a decade later, in 1967-68, Local 35 paid the expenses for the ill-fated "Association of C&Ts" (ACT). The ACT campaign lasted for a few years, but with the exception of a handful of departments, the Association was unable to generate significant interest among the rank and file. Subsequently, a group of the ACT leaders formed an organization independent of Local 35—the Yale Non-Faculty Action Committee (YNFAC). The YNFAC drive climaxed with an NLRB election in 1971, in which the union lost by a 2-1 margin.

Like the ACT campaign, the YNFAC drive suffered from an inability to develop a large rank-and-file organizing committee capable of communicating with the diverse groups of employees spread throughout the vast University system. While the organization was strong in several departments, it was unable to mount an effective campus-wide effort. The University ran a strong anti-union campaign, relying primarily on hundreds of work time "captive audience" meetings of small groups of employees. At these meetings, University representatives argued that a union would only mean high dues, strikes, and a loss of control by the C&Ts over their own work lives.

Several years after the YNFAC drive failed, the Office and Professional Employees International Union (OPEIU) made an attempt to organize the C&Ts at Yale. The University, assuming that its white collar workers were no longer interested in forming a union, did not this time make much of an effort to conduct an anti-union campaign. Perhaps due to this complacency, the union came within a few hundred votes of winning certification in 1977. Encouraged by the closeness of the vote, the OPEIU continued organizing among the C&Ts and the UAW began a campaign of its own on the Yale campus. While the OPEIU dropped out in 1979, the UAW devoted several more years to organizing at Yale. For almost a year and a half, the Auto Workers competed with the nascent Local 34 for the support of the clericals and technicals. The UAW withdrew from the scene in January 1982, leaving the field exclusively to Local 34.

Like the ACT effort of 1967-68, the Local 34 drive enjoyed the full support, financial and otherwise, of Local 35. The service and maintenance workers' decision to support an organizing drive among the clericals and technicals represented not only an abstract feeling of solidarity with their co-workers, but also a realization by them of the practical necessity of organizing other segments of the University work force. Standing alone, Local 35 did not have sufficient leverage to stand up to Yale.

Local 35 had itself been in existence in one form or another since the late 1930s, when the workers in the Grounds Maintenance Department (mostly groundskeepers) had organized and affiliated themselves with the United Mine Workers. Over the next three decades, employees in several additional departments of the University joined the blue collar union. Until 1968, Local 35 peacefully coexisted with the University, foregoing higher wages and other benefits in exchange for flexible work rules and a decent work environment. In 1968, however, according to John Wilhelm, the union's business manager, the University "came down on Local 35 like a ton of bricks."

In that year, Yale hired new personnel administrators who set out to exert greater control over the union. The new administrators, for instance, adopted a policy for granting sick leave under which no member of Local 35 could receive sick pay without being at home on the days when unable to come to work. Thus an employee who could not work because of a disability such as a broken leg might not be medically required to be confined indoors, but could not receive sick pay unless he or she were at home to answer the telephone when management called to check up. Such management practices fueled enormous resentment among the workers.

In response to Yale's new hard-line approach to its labor relations Local 35 went out on strike in 1968, 1971, 1974, and 1977; that is— each time its contract ran out within the decade. The 1971 strike ended with a bloody confrontation between the New Haven police and strikers on Yale's graduation day. The adverse publicity which Yale received from the incident helped the union gain a victory which brought its members raises of 33% over the three-year contract. However, each successive strike in the 1970s was longer than its predecessor, and the 1977 walkout lasted over three months. In all its strikes not a single Local 35 member scabbed, but it was becoming apparent to the leaders of the union that by themselves, the service and maintenance workers did not have enough leverage to bargain successfully with the University without paying an increasingly heavy price.

Local 35 therefore gave its support to the 1977 OPEIU drive with both solidarity and its own interests in mind. And when the UAW showed an interest in organizing the C&Ts, John Wilhelm told that union's organizers that the blue collar workers were behind them. However, the UAW organizers responded by telling Wilhelm that they thought it would be useful to keep some distance between the white collar workers and their blue collar co-workers, and essentially turned down Local 35's offer of support. When the OPEIU and UAW drives failed to take off, Local 35 decided that they had no choice but to try to organize the C&Ts themselves.

Local 35 quickly exploited some advantages it held over the previous unions that had attempted organizing drives among the C&Ts. First, Local 35 had a reputation, as Wilhelm describes it, as a union that was "reasonably effective, reasonably democratic, and was one which had stood up to the University." Many of the pro-union C&Ts had already asked Local 35's leaders to sponsor a drive.

According to one C&T, a lifetime resident of New Haven, when Local 35 finally did decide to get involved with organizing Local 34, it was like "a dream come true."

The second major advantage which Local 35 enjoyed and employed was its extensive set of contacts in the community. New Haven has been likened to a company town; most families include at least one person who works for Yale. The union therefore began its drive by asking each member of Local 35 for the names and addresses of, and introductions to, friends, relatives, and neighbors who worked at Yale as C&Ts. The union eventually got several leads on potential members. In fact, the original group contacted by Local 34 evolved into the core of the union's rank-and-file organizing committee.

Local 35 supported the new union in several other ways as well. First, they lent John Wilhelm to Local 34. Throughout the drive he served as Local 34's chief organizer and later as its chief negotiator. Moreover, the members of Local 35 voted twice to raise their own dues so that they could assist financially in the organizing drive. The blue collar workers chose to contribute to the organizing drive even though many of them were still resentful about the fact that most C&Ts had crossed Local 35's picket lines during their four previous strikes. That so many members of Local 34's rank-and-file organizing committee had been referred by members of Local 35 helped both unions to avoid the potential problem of residual bitterness.

And finally, Local 35 brought to the campaign the strong financial support of its International, the Hotel and Restaurant Employees. Beginning in the mid-1970s, the International granted a special subsidy to its New England district for training new organizers, many of whom eventually worked on the Yale drive. The International also contributed over $2 million to the campaign and another million during the strike itself.

When the drive began officially in November 1980, Local 34's organizers believed that one of their first responsibilities was to stimulate discussion among the C&Ts about how a union could affect their work lives. They encouraged employees to abandon preconceptions about what unions do and how they operate. The organizers told the workers that Local 34 could be whatever its members wanted it to be, and could take on whatever issues the members cared about.

This strategy was consistent with the views of John Wilhelm, perhaps the drive's chief architect, who asserts that to be most effective, paid organizers should not make promises about what the union will do for the workers; instead they should concentrate on developing a strong rank-and-file organizing committee that "knows what it's talking about" and is able to gain the trust of fellow employees. People should then be organized, Wilhelm argues, "around the notion that the union is a tool for them to use to deal with whatever they want to, as opposed to insurance policy unionism, where you say, 'Well, if you join the union, you'll get fifty cents an hour more,' or 'If you join the union, we'll have good health and welfare,' which I don't think works very well."

In contrast to previous organizing drives at Yale, Local 34 rejected the use of literature for the first year of its drive, made no efforts to get members to sign union cards for over a year and a half, and concentrated at first exclusively on building not the membership, but the organizing committee. This strategy was not received without skepticism by some of Local 34's supporters, who were surprised by the union's failure to put out position papers as part of its organizing campaign. As Wilhelm recalls, "We had to persuade people that the only way to beat the University had nothing to do with literature, and had nothing to do with issues, as people normally conceive of them, although everybody has plenty of issues. But if we were going to beat the University, we had to have a gigantic organizing committee."

The union's organizers believed that it was counterproductive to rely on literature as an organizing tool since position papers reflect only the author's point of view, but cannot respond to each individual worker's particular reservations about getting involved. As Warren Heyman, a member of Local 34's paid organizing staff, argues, literature should not be relied upon to organize since "a piece of paper only raises questions; it doesn't answer any questions. You can only get someone to understand what a union is about by talking to them." Or as Aldo Cupo, one of the union's earliest rank-and-file organizers puts it, one of the main jobs of an organizer is to help people to overcome their doubts, and no piece of literature can answer people's fears. Therefore leaflets "should never be used as a substitute for a conversation."

In keeping with their strategy of simply "talking union," Local 34's supporters tried to discuss the drive with their co-workers whenever and wherever possible. The organizers held lunch meetings, set up meetings after work, visited employees' homes, and even organized house parties at which the workers could get together to talk about the union. The first year of the drive was occupied almost exclusively with such meetings and phone calls to supplement those meetings.

At first, the paid organizers relied upon rank-and-file supporters to set up meetings with their co-workers, although the union staff members ran the meetings. Eventually the rank-and-filers were expected to play a large part in running the meetings. The confidence of many of the active members increased as they saw that they were capable of having effective discussions with their peers. Deborah Chernoff recalls that when she was first approached by the union, she said that she would be "happy to help—to stuff envelopes or run the printing press." She lacked the confidence, however, to speak out at large gatherings or to run small group discussions. But the union's organizers kept pushing her to set up lunch meetings and to speak to her co-workers, and Chernoff began to realize that she could assume a position of responsibility in Local 34.

From the beginning, Local 34 organizers stressed that taking responsibility was an essential part of belonging to a union. The paid staff repeatedly pointed out that Local 34 could be successful only if the members regarded it as their union. When one of the organizers first approached Beverly Lett, "He didn't say, 'Just sign a card.' What he said was, 'I want you to do some work. I want you to help, because it's going to be your union, not my union, because I'm going to be gone some day.'" Aldo Cupo received a similar message. As Rob Traber, one of the paid staffers, told him at their initial meeting, "If you really want a union, you're going to have to work for it."

The paid organizers' insistence that the rank and file assume significant responsibility for organizing the union was not always accepted without resistance. As Chernoff recalls, "At first I resented the idea that we were expected to do the work ourselves. I thought that having a union on campus meant you had organizers, and they called meetings and gave you information and you signed a card; if they wanted to sign somebody up 'they' signed that person up. I remember thinking, 'Why should they ask us to do that? That's their job.' But after I'd been dragged to a few meetings, I began to think that actually it was kind of interesting that we would have some control over the process and that they wanted to give people leadership roles."

The paid organizers concentrated their efforts on recruiting rank-and-filers and training them to be organizers themselves. In fact, in contrast to most other unions which often reserve the title "organizer" for the members of their professional staff, Local 34 began to refer to the most active members as the "rank-and-file organizers" or the "unpaid staff." As Warren Heyman explains, "The principal role of the professional organizers was to figure out who the leadership was within the work force and then to train them in the skills of being an organizer." The paid and unpaid organizers also taught each other by regularly critiquing the progress of the drive and going over organizing techniques.

The reliance on rank-and-file organizers was necessitated by the fact that Yale's C&T work force of approximately two thousand six hundred employees was spread out in some 250 campus buildings. Work groups often consisted of two to four people, and it was a rarity to find an office or laboratory with over ten workers. Given the fragmentation of the work force, the organizers had no choice but to attempt to secure at least one strong union supporter in every office. As one paid staffer remarked, at a place like Yale, "thirty people simply can't organize 2600."

Even the planners of the drive were not entirely sure what form the committee structure would take or how it would function. The organizers thought that if they could recruit 250 C&Ts to the Organizing Committee, it would be capable of reaching all the offices and labs. Eventually they came to believe that 550 was the number of organizers needed, but they were never able to recruit more than 450 rank-and-filers. As the Organizing Committee grew, it became too unwieldy for certain purposes, such as high-level strategizing. The result was the spawning of the "Steering Committee," which had approximately 150 members and met once a week. The members of the Steering Committee generally had responsibility for working with three to four members of the Organizing Committee as well as with the C&Ts in their own work group. When even the Steering Committee became too large, there evolved the "Rank-and-File Staff," which had approximately fifty-five to sixty members who were responsible for training several members of the Steering Committee, as well as for working with the Organizing Committee and their own work group. All the committees were open to any member who was willing to make the time-commitment necessary to fulfill the many responsibilities of being a leader of the union. This committee structure helped ensure that the union was run democratically.

The Local 34 organizers planned a "positive" campaign, stressing the advantages of union organization rather than the disadvantages of working at Yale. Thus Local 34 sought to project the union as a vehicle through which the C&Ts could gain respect and recognition for their work, as opposed to simply a mechanism for obtaining higher wages or better benefits. Using this strategy, the union made it harder for the University to co-opt its issues by, for example, granting a raise during the drive. Local 34, from the inception of the drive, eschewed organizing around specific issues and instead organized around the fact that the University had continually demonstrated a lack of respect for the C&Ts and their work. While the organizers did recognize that the members wanted to attain some specific goals, such as higher wages and better medical benefits, they argued that the poor compensation and working conditions which the clericals and technicals had experienced were themselves only manifestations of the University's general lack of respect for the C&Ts' work. Even though the University did grant a wage increase at the beginning of the Local 34 drive in an effort to make the Union seem unnecessary, that increase was not considered satisfactory to most workers nor could it address the employees' demand for more respect and a greater voice in the workplace.

The reasons why people decided to join the union were as diverse as the C&Ts who got involved in the drive. Rosamond Hamlin joined Local 34 because almost immediately after going to work at Yale, she began to feel that she was being "treated like a serf and not recognized as a human being." Beverly Lett became active in the drive largely because she objected to the way she saw supervisors treating the people she worked with. Andrea Ross turned to the union because she was shocked that some of her co-workers, who had been working at Yale for almost twenty years, were making only $600 per year more than she was for the same kind of work. Ross recalls thinking that two options were open to her: she could either leave Yale and find work elsewhere or she "could join the union and change things, and I decided that that is what I had to do." And Aldo Cupo decided to become involved after his request for a raise was never even answered by his supervisor.

The union never presumed to define for the workers the difficulties associated with working at Yale. Where the working conditions are poor, says John Wilhelm, "virtually everybody knows there are problems." It is therefore not necessary, he adds, for the organizers to try to convince the workers that, for instance, their salaries are too low or that their contribution is not recognized. Rather, what the union must do is "persuade people that it's possible to improve those things, and secondly, that the union is the best way to improve them . . . . You have to persuade people of both of those things."

The organizers' aggressiveness in addressing the reservations of the C&Ts about unions prevented the University from relying on one of the mainstays of the conventional anti-union campaign: painting the organizers as outsiders concerned only with the collection of dues. The constant participation of the employees in their own drive made Yale's "outsider" accusation appear to be disingenuous and self-interested. And Local 34 demonstrated the union's good faith and defused the dues issue by pledging not to collect any initiation fees or dues until a first contract had been secured. In addition, Local 34's commitment to allow the members to set their own dues and initiation fees further undermined the University's argument that the union was just after the C&T's money.

The union countered Yale's use of other tactics by anticipating them and preparing the C&Ts to be ready for them. Local 34 effectively pre-empted the use of captive audience meetings by publicly taking the position that the coercion inherent in such meetings would be contrary to the University's stated commitment to freedom of expression. Local 34 prepared the rank-and-file organizers by holding Saturday workshops, attended by 400-500 members of the Organizing Committee, at which the paid staff participated in mock captive audience meetings, sessions on how to organize, and role-playing to provide practice in confronting supervisors and anti-union C&Ts with arguments for the union. The union also distributed copies of University literature from previous campaigns. When the University sent out one of its managers to hold lunchtime meetings with C&Ts as part of a series called "Let's Talk," Local 34 packed the meetings with union activists.

A particular example of the union's ability to anticipate the administration's arguments concerned the so-called "mob issue." Local 34 organizers were well aware that allegations had been made of connections between their International—the Hotel and Restaurant Employees' Union—and organized crime. Rather than wait for Yale to bring up these charges during the drive in an effort to smear the union and discredit the organizing campaign, the union organizers themselves introduced the issue to the members of the bargaining unit by showing the Organizing Committee a videotape of an NBC News report on the accusations, and by distributing copies of news articles which had been written on the subject. The union, as one member of the rank-and-file staff put it, "innoculated the Organizing Committee about the mob stuff in the beginning," and diminished the University's ability to make the charges an issue in the drive, while reinforcing trust in the honesty of the local's leadership.

Local 34 finally petitioned for an election in early 1983, and continued to organize during the National Labor Relations Board (NLRB) hearings held to determine which C&Ts could vote in the union election. During the hearings, the union's organizers seized every opportunity to make an issue of Yale's tactics, not only to encourage employees to join Local 34, but also to organize support for the drive among the other members of the Yale community.

During previous campaigns, the University had quickly agreed to the proposed bargaining units since they were convinced that no clerical union could win a certification election anyway. But at the hearings in February 1983, Yale adopted a strategy of stalling. The University began the hearings by submitting a list of 300 proposed witnesses, and informed the Board of its intention to call even more later on: Yale's goal was to stretch out the hearing process by calling large numbers of employees and claiming that under federal labor law they were in fact supervisory personnel and therefore could not be in the union. This appeared to be a wise tactic for the University not only because it would frustrate the workers' desire to have an election as soon as possible, but also because of the special nature of the University's academic calendar. During the summer months, the University virtually shuts down, and many of its employees leave their jobs. Yale's administration seemed to be acting on the belief that if it could delay the election until the fall, the union would have lost many of its supporters due to the summer turnover, and would be faced with the prospect of large numbers of new hires unfamiliar with the union. However, Local 34 anticipated this strategy and, rather than waiting out the delays or simply complaining to the NLRB, came up with an organizing program to embarrass the University and compel it to abandon its stalling tactics.

Local 34 turned Yale's plan against the University by bringing C&Ts to the hearings to witness their employer's delays and to hear Yale's argument that particular employees who had absolutely no supervisory responsibilities were actually "management personnel." Most of the workers who went to the hearings were outraged by what they perceived as the University's attempt to deny them the right to vote.

Many who attended went back to their workplaces and told their co-workers of Yale's tactics. In addition, the union distributed a leaflet throughout the Yale campus which included the reactions of several C&Ts who had observed the hearings. As one union member who had attended the proceedings remarked, "Yale was condescending, manipulative, devious, and outright insulting to the clericals and technicals as a group.'' Another C&T called the University's stalling tactics "disgraceful.'' As a result of the union's efforts to expose the University's stalling, many people at Yale were soon convinced that the administration was acting in bad faith. As Beverly Lett recalls, "We got everybody, even anti-union people, upset at how the University was stalling. We had the whole campus saying, 'People have the right to vote. Why don't you give the C&Ts the right to vote?' Soon afterwards, the University stopped its stalling."

The union also effectively made an issue out of the location of the NLRB hearings. Under Board rules, hearings are to be held in the NLRB regional office (in this case in Hartford, forty miles from New Haven) unless both the employer and the union agree to have the hearings in another location. The University insisted on holding the hearings in Hartford, which made it difficult for members of the Yale community to attend. Local 34's organizers argued that Yale resisted the relocation of the proceedings in order to hide their delaying tactics.

In March 1983, Local 34 circulated among the entire Yale community—students, faculty, and employees—a petition supporting the C&Ts' "Right to Vote." The petition represented one of the union's first attempts to go outside the bargaining unit and organize support among the rest of the campus. As a result of the union's agitation, the administration suffered embarrassment, and finally agreed to allow the hearings to be held in New Haven. Soon thereafter, Yale said that it would call no more witnesses, in effect agreeing to a prompt election. The union had won its right to an election before the summer turnover, and in the process had diminished the credibility of the University and increased its own strength at the same time.

Union activists had to contend every day with both subtle and overt harassment by unsympathetic supervisors. Probably the most blatant acts of attempted intimidation occurred in the medical area of the University. "In the medical school," Kim McLaughlin recalls, "the supervisors would outright tell people that if they joined the union, they would fire them." The doctors seemed to be exceptionally hostile to union activists whom they supervised, a fact which

McLaughlin attributes to the doctors' professional standing: "Many of them are world-renowned experts and they think they own the world. They treat their employees and their secretaries and particularly their lab technicians like peons."

In addition to the overt threats, medical area supervisors and doctors tried to pressure union activists by accusing them of both personal disloyalty and a lack of concern for patients. It was not an easy thing for the C&Ts simply to shrug off these remarks. Kim McLaughlin believed that the problem was particularly acute with women workers. She held that a unique difficulty facing organizers dealing with female workers is that "women in our society are socially conditioned to try and please everybody. We're the great compromisers, and try to make sure that we're not too assertive about our own rights or needs."

The union staff tried to counteract the pressure from supervisors by encouraging the Organizing Committee members to give each other emotional support. Local 34 members were regularly reassured by their peers that participation in the union was perfectly consistent with their responsibility to their patients and their co-workers. After bolstering each other's spirits, Local 34 activists frequently would go after a hostile boss by organizing a petition drive or holding a small demonstration in that supervisor's office. This often put the supervisor on the defensive, at least temporarily. In one instance, a rank-and-file organizer, who worked as a laboratory technician and had a reputation for being an excellent worker, was told by her supervisor that she was taking too many breaks. One morning her co-workers brought signs to work, and when she took her first break, they all put signs around their necks saying "Joan Smith is on break." The organizers often found that mocking the boss was the most effective way to support each other.

Local 34 also built confidence among C&Ts by publicly showing the growing numbers of workers who had already joined the union. The union in the fall of 1981 issued its first major piece of literature—a leaflet entitled "Standing Together," which was essentially a list bearing the names of approximately 450 of the union supporters and an explanation of why they had decided to form a union. Shortly after that, the union held its first rally, attended by some 500-600 people. The rally featured colored balloons and a brass band which led a spirited march from the center of the Yale campus to a nearby church where the rally was being held. Participation in the rally signified a public commitment to the union, and was therefore a big step to take. The C&Ts from the medical area had to take buses to the part of the campus where the rally took place and, as Aldo Cupo relates it, "To go on the bus was telling the boss 'I'm for the union and I'm going to the rally'." The demonstration took a month to organize, but after it had been held, it was easier to sign up new members and to persuade existing members to take public pro-union positions, since afterwards, as Cupo remembers, "People had a sense of joining a very visible, very tough, and winning team."

The union also used its leaflets to satirize the positions taken by University officials. Wilhelm, who often authored such literature, was fond of quoting from statements made by Yale President A. Bartlett Giamatti in order to make the point that the University's anti-union actions frequently ran counter to Giamatti's grandiose rhetoric. For instance, the union in February 1983 inaugurated a series of leaflets entitled "Full and Open Discussion." The bulletin's title was derived from a statement of President Giamatti that he "fully supported the right of the clerical and technical staff to decide [whether or not to vote union] after full and open discussion of the issues." The union literature suggested, and union organizers asserted, that the University's effort to keep the NLRB hearings in Hartford was designed to prevent just such an "open discussion," and that Yale's delaying tactics were intended to frustrate the staff's right "to decide."

After two and a half years of hard work, the certification election was finally held on May 18, 1983. On the day of the election, union activists worked to get out every pro-union vote they could find: driving to the polls people who had not worked that day and in one case even picking up a member at the airport in order to bring her to vote before the polls closed. Many of the rank-and-file staff had thought that the union would win by 100-200 votes, but the actual vote proved far closer than that. During the counting of the ballots, for quite some time the union trailed, and then for several hours the results seesawed; one minute, a union victory seemed certain, while the next, the union's chances seemed hopeless. For many of those waiting for the results, the tension was too much to take, and it was not possible to stay in the room and hear the tallies being taken.

Finally, at approximately 10:30 P.M., after more than four hours of counting the ballots, the tallying was over. In the silent auditorium the crowd anxiously watched the Board officials add up the totals. However, before the results could be announced Wilhelm made any such announcement superfluous, bowing his head from exhaustion but at the same time raising both hands over his head in the traditional boxer's victory salute.

Wilhelm's gesture touched off a tumultuous celebration among the union supporters present. Many began to cry, others started jumping up and down, clapping their hands, stomping their feet, or embracing their friends. Finally, as if to steal a scene from the film *Norma Rae*, the crowd began to chant, over and over again, "Union, Union, Union."

Out of a total of 2,505 ballots cast, Local 34 had prevailed by the incredibly slim margin of 39 votes, with 33 of those votes subject to challenge. The union had won with only 50.9% of the votes cast, but the margin of victory was not all that important for the moment: All that mattered was that after thirty years of struggle, Yale University's clerical and technical employees had finally won a union. They would soon learn that that achievement was quite a different thing from winning a first contract.

Negotiating with Yale

Following Local 34's victory in the certification election, many union members held the hope that Yale would come to accept their organization's legitimate place on campus. Such optimism grew as a result of the post-election statement of President Giamatti that "It is now time to put aside our differences and in good faith to work together." In this climate of anticipation, the new union prepared to bargain for its first contract.

The way in which Local 34 drew up its initial bargaining positions reflected the democratic decision-making process that the union had adopted during its organizing drive. Members came together at hundreds of small-group meetings throughout the summer of 1983, soliciting and discussing contract proposals. According to Local 34 member Andrea Ross, many C&Ts at first expressed doubts at those meetings regarding their ability to draw up negotiating demands: People felt "How can we possibly talk about contract proposals when none of us has ever seen a union contract before? How can we talk about what has to be in it? But then we started gradually to realize that all we had to do was to examine very carefully our work-lives here at Yale and how we would change them in order to make them better."

After the small group meetings, the next step in the contract framing was circulation of two rounds of surveys to all clerical and technical workers, union members and non-members alike, asking which issues they considered most important. Almost 2,000 employees responded, including many who were not yet union members. This open procedure for drawing up the contract produced "an enormous upsurge in membership," recalled Ross; workers appreciated that "they had an active role in putting the proposals together." In August and September, a 500-member Contract Committee (formerly the union's Organizing Committee) hammered out preliminary contract proposals based on the surveys. Some of the contract issues were sent to special committees for formulation. The retirement proposals, for example, were drawn up by a group of long-term C&Ts. The next step in the process was a mass meeting attended by over 1,100 clerical and technical employees. At this meeting, the membership adopted the Contract Committee's list of bargaining proposals, voted to have John Wilhelm serve as Local 34's chief negotiator, and set up procedures for the election of a negotiating committee.

On October 3 and 4, secret ballot elections were held throughout the University by which C&Ts selected a 35-member negotiating committee, which had representatives from all areas of the campus and even included members who had not joined the union until after its victory in the NLRB election. The size of the committee, criticized by the administration as unwieldy, facilitated communications between the rank and file and the contract bargainers.

Sharply contrasting with Giamatti's pledge to negotiate seriously with Local 34 were University actions immediately after the election. Yale dropped its local lawyers and hired the Chicago-based firm of Seyfarth, Shaw, Fairweather and Geraldson, labeled by the AFL-CIO as one of the most notorious anti-union law firms in the country. Seyfarth, Shaw had acquired its reputation by using the management-provoked strike as a weapon against newly certified unions. Its standard approach was to persuade clients to avoid serious negotiations with unions and then at the eleventh hour to make an offer known to be unacceptable to them. This tactic forced the unions to strike and risk defeat before solidifying their membership.

Considering Yale's employment of Seyfarth, Shaw, it is perhaps no surprise that the University appointed a negotiating committee that had no power to bargain effectively with the union. In addition to Seyfarth, Shaw lawyer Jay Swardensky, the Yale side included seven lower-level administrators and faculty members. During negotiations, Swardensky repeatedly requested a recess so he could cross campus to confer with Bruce Chrisman, the University's vice-president in charge of administration, who in turn briefed President Giamatti after each session of negotiations.

Yale's relations with Local 35 hardened during the same time period. In Fall 1983, Local 35 chief steward Phil Voigt charged that the University had forced over 150 of the blue-collar union's grievances into formal arbitration hearings, neglecting lower-level procedures which were less formalized, less expensive, and less plodding. The practical result of such management policies, Voigt claimed, was to clog the grievance procedure channels and frustrate his union's effort to protect its members.

These indications that the course of contract negotiations would not be smooth were confirmed as soon as bargaining began on October 19, 1983. The Yale negotiators, citing the size of the Local 34 team, claimed that the campus of 250 buildings had no available room large enough to seat all of the bargainers comfortably. The two sides were thereby forced to repair to a church in the vicinity to conduct negotiations. Further, Yale refused to pay the members of Local 34's bargaining committee for time spent in negotiations, although for years they had compensated negotiators for Local 35.

New troubles surfaced in negotiations when the University presented a comprehensive economic proposal to the union on January 10, 1984. Before that time, the two sides had argued only over such issues as grievance procedures and job security; now economic questions entered the discussion as well. Local 34's initial economic demands, presented in December, had addressed the types of pay structure issues that its members had indicated as a high priority. Across-the-board increases were sought, to be implemented in yearly stages over the course of the contract. The union also called for a system of ''step'' increases—salary levels that employees would climb up year by year within their job classifications—and for ''slotting,'' which would place existing employees at the pay level they would have been in had the step system already been in place.

The step system was proposed as a way to provide a regular promotion path for clerical and technical workers at Yale. Since C&Ts would receive some salary advancement automatically, a step system would decrease the extent to which future workers at Yale found themselves stranded with low salaries. Such a mechanism would not overcome salary discrimination on its own; nothing would compel Yale to promote C&Ts to higher job categories as they became more experienced. Slotting, for its part, would repair some of the effects of past pay discrimination against long-term employees. It would help replace the arbitrariness that had become widespread in the absence of an explicit promotion policy. It would address a situation in which men tended to be concentrated in better paying jobs, despite women's greater seniority. In effect, slotting would retroactively institute a seniority system and narrow the gap between men's and women's salaries.

These various proposals sought to restructure the salary system in a complex, yet ordered, fashion. The slotting would help undo past discrimination against women and long-time workers; the steps would help prevent the discrimination from recurring. Across-the-board increases, which received the most attention, would improve the level of clerical and technical salaries as a whole.

The administration initially rejected both the step and slotting proposals and instead offered across-the-board pay raises to all C&Ts and a system of "merit pay" increases for those workers judged most efficient by management. Throughout the negotiations, the University claimed that it could not afford to agree to the union's demands, citing a spending rule adopted by the Yale Corporation in 1977 to ensure that the real value of its endowment remained intact over time. Local 34 countered with its own analysis of Yale's financial resources, arguing that the University had amassed a large budget *surplus* in the previous fiscal year and therefore was fully capable of paying its clerical and technical workers decent salaries. However, debating the merits of each side's economic case was not the centerpiece of Local 34's strategy. The union's economic arguments were not marshaled primarily to convince the Yale administration of the virtues of Local 34's proposals, but rather to enlist support among the Yale and New Haven communities. The union contended that the University's economic arguments were a pretext to avoid serious negotiations. According to Steve Fortes, a member of Local 34's Negotiating Committee, the University's strategy seemed to be "to outlast and to demoralize us.''

The union's style of negotiating helped to prevent such an outcome. Local 34 acted on the conviction that the negotiating process did not take place in a vacuum; rather, the give and take of bargaining was a product of the external pressures brought to bear on both sides in the dispute. Or, as Andrea Ross put it, the members of the union team frequently reminded themselves that the ''negotiations did not take place in that room,'' but instead, ''back in the offices and the labs.'' The union membership was able to respond in a cohesive manner to the University's bargaining strategy because the union's negotiators saw their essential responsibility to be to communicate with the rank-and-file and to work with them to devise a collective response. As Steve Fortes recalls, the principal function of each Negotiating Committee member was ''pretty much what it always had been, to be an organizer.'' For this reason, Local 34 felt no need to include lawyers or other ''experts'' on its negotiating team.

As it had during the certification drive, Local 34 turned Yale's stalling tactics into an organizing tool both within the membership and in the broader community. Local 34 made a major issue of Yale's decision to hire the Seyfarth, Shaw law firm, which was well known for its strategies of frustrating the negotiating process. The union distributed throughout the campus a pamphlet entitled *Yale's Labor Law Firm*, detailing the history of Seyfarth, Shaw. The pamphlet's cover reproduced a telling statement from one of the Seyfarth, Shaw partners, boasting that the firm subscribed to ''the bomb-them-into-submission school of labor relations.''

The union also invited to Yale a labor leader who was all too familiar with Seyfarth, Shaw—United Farm Workers President Cesar Chavez. Chavez's mid-February appearance signified for many that Local 34 was part of a labor tradition that embodied idealistic, grassroots unionism as well as the spirit and tactics of a moral crusade. Chavez posed the question to a packed house: ''How can a prestigious university which cultivates an image of enlightenment— and sometimes even liberalism—make book with the worst union-busting firm in the land?'' After pointing out that his own union had frequently encountered Seyfarth, Shaw lawyers representing California growers, Chavez warned Yale workers that this firm "knows more than any negotiators we have ever met how to keep negotiations going, how to stall for time, how to double talk, all the gimmicks to prolong negotiations. . . . It is almost impossible to get contracts with them. . .and if by some luck we get a contract signed, they're already organizing. . .to throw the union out."

To protest the slow pace of negotiations, Local 34 mobilized its membership for a dramatic demonstration. In early February, approximately 1,200 members of Local 34 and their campus supporters braved freezing weather to hold an hour-long vigil outside President Giamatti's house following work hours. Carrying flashlights and candles, the demonstrators stood in complete silence. This vigil was to be the first of several large-scale demonstrations organized by Local 34 in the year to come which would confirm the belief among C&Ts and their supporters that they were participating in a cause with a deep moral purpose.

Meanwhile, President Giamatti publicly defended Yale's bargaining position. At a student forum he criticized the union for putting forward "charming but unreasonable" demands and creating "phony issues" regarding the slow pace of the negotiating process. "Collective bargaining," Giamatti quipped, "is not a picnic."

The union responded to Giamatti's charges that its bargaining position was unreasonable. At a mass meeting on March 1st the members of Local 34 voted 1,309 to 165 to propose that the two sides submit all unsettled issues to binding arbitration. In addition, the members voted to set a March 28 strike deadline. Within 45 minutes of the meeting, Yale officials rejected the proposal for binding arbitration. In a later press release, Yale vice-president Chrisman contended that the contract should be negotiated by the University and the union, "not some third party who in the time allowed may not come to know the intricacies of the situation. We must remain in control of the university."

There was considerable dismay among Yale's staff, students, and faculty that the University had not accepted arbitration as a means to avoid the disruption and ill-will that a strike on campus would surely bring. The union used Yale's rejection of arbitration to question whether the administration truly thought that it was the union's proposals which were "unreasonable." John Wilhelm said: "The air of their response reminds me of Nero fiddling while Rome burned. If their proposals are so justified, why won't they let a neutral professional arbitrate?"

Union supporters among students and faculty circulated petitions calling upon the administration either to settle or to arbitrate; almost 250 of the faculty and several thousand students signed. These efforts were among the most successful in organizing supporters of Local 34 into *ad hoc* groups that would grow in size as the possibility of a strike increased. The concept of arbitration remained popular on campus even after negotiations broke down and a strike began. A widely sung picket-line tune during the subsequent strike put the question to Yale: "If you will not arbitrate, why don't you negotiate?"

To demonstrate both the union's demand for a fair contract and the broad support in the Yale and New Haven communities for Local 34, the union sponsored a public rally on March 8. Held in front of the administration building where the Yale Corporation had scheduled a meeting, this demonstration was also timed to coincide with International Women's Day in order to highlight the special problems of a work force that was predominantly female. The union's flyer invited the people of New Haven to attend the rally "because Yale University sets the standard for salaries of clerical and technical workers throughout the city." The flyer continued, "If Local 34 loses this struggle for a fair contract, all salaries in New Haven will be held down. Come out for yourselves and Local 34." Despite unseasonably cold weather, more than 4,000 people, many carrying handmade placards and banners, turned out. Representatives of a number of New Haven labor unions and women's groups joined speakers from Local 34 and Local 35 in calling on the Yale administration to bargain in good faith.

President Giamatti dismissed the rally and other recent union activities as media stunts: "I hope after the union has finished with its petitions, vigils, banners, and rallies, it will come back to the bargaining table with its 50 observers and negotiate," said Giamatti. "If the union chooses to manipulate the press and use students as pawns to pressure the University, that's fine. But we do not believe in such tactics. That's not negotiating in good faith at the bargaining table.''

As negotiations stretched out over many months, the union began to believe that a few key members of the Yale Corporation held real power in setting the University's bargaining position. J. Richardson Dilworth, John Madden, and Cyrus Vance came to be regarded by Wilhelm and other union members as the principal opponents on the Corporation of significant concessions to the union. Noting that these three men as well as other Corporation members served on the boards of many large banks and companies, Beverly Lett, one of the Local 34 negotiators, charged that the Corporation was controlled primarily by businessmen "with the priorities of business people." Corporation members with reputations for liberal views on social and political issues, members such as civil rights lawyer Eleanor Holmes Norton and Episcopal bishop Paul Moore, were thought to have been "co-opted" by the University. Wilhelm also noted that the firms on whose boards the power brokers on the Yale Corporation sat had in recent years forced their unions to make significant concessions in contract bargaining and therefore underestimated the strength of a new, predominantly female union.

As negotiations wore on without progress, workers began to discuss the possibility of a walkout. Andrea Ross recalled that throughout the fall and winter members had been afraid even to mention the potential for a strike, but by the spring more and more C&Ts began using the euphemism "S word." After setting a March 28 strike deadline, the union distributed a pamphlet on March 6 requesting all members of the Yale community to support their "struggle for dignity."

The disruptive potential of a strike loomed larger in mid-March, when Local 35 members made known their willingness to honor Local 34's picket lines in the event that the C&Ts walked off their jobs. Their position was perhaps not surprising given the fact that John Wilhelm served as Local 34's chief negotiator and as Local 35's business agent. Without the services of the blue-collar workers the students' food service would shut down and cleaning and maintenance would come to a halt. The University sent letters to the union, warning that any such action would violate the no-strike clause in its contract and similarly moved to head off sympathetic actions by faculty members and teaching assistants.

As the strike deadline approached, students and faculty reacted in a variety of ways. Most undergraduate students were gravely concerned about how the strike would affect their lives. Many were reported to be pilfering dining hall food, china, and silverware in anticipation that dining hall workers would honor Local 34 picket lines. At the same time, a small but active minority of students, together with faculty sympathizers, conducted the preparations of a different nature. At the Yale Women's Center, union sympathizers prepared literature explaining the union's grievances and found locations off-campus for more than 300 classes whose students or instructors wanted to avoid crossing picket lines. At the Yale Law School, students addressed a public letter to President Giamatti, warning that the administration's failure to "bargain seriously" with Local 34 threatened to erode alumni financial support. John Trinkaus, a biology professor sympathetic to Local 34, denounced the University's economic offer before a campus rally as evidence of "a mean, stingy management, whose shabby approach is to conform to the standard American exploitation of women and blacks and all others who find themselves in clerical and technical jobs." On the day before the strike deadline, pro-union female students, carrying bread and roses, sponsored a "woman's vigil" stressing the feminist issues involved in the bargaining.

A different manifestation of campus tensions in the days before the strike deadline surfaced in a campaign conducted by a minority of clerical and technical workers who tried to pressure the administration to resist Local 34's call for a union shop. Two of these workers wrote a letter to the campus newspaper complaining that "formerly reasonable, pleasant [pro-union] colleagues" were "becoming obnoxious and pesky," and they asked that the University protect their "right to an open shop." While 300 Local 34 members held a silent vigil outside, a smaller number of anti-union C&Ts met on March 26, just two days before the strike deadline, to discuss the possibility of a decertification campaign.

As the strike deadline drew near, the first significant progress at the bargaining table occurred. On March 16, both sides agreed to contract language regarding health and safety protection comparable to Local 35's and on grievance procedures that included final recourse to outside arbitration. These breakthroughs raised widespread hopes, but little further progress was made when bargaining turned to economic issues and employee promotion and transfer policies. In an attempt to avert a strike, both sides agreed to invite a federal mediator to attend negotiating sessions. With the mediator present, a compromise solution was hammered out on March 26 on the controversial issue of the "open shop." The union proposed an "agency shop" under which workers would not have to join the union so long as they contributed to a fund, jointly supervised by the University and Local 34, to finance the costs of administering the contract. To the surprise of many on the union negotiating team, Yale's bargainers accepted this proposal. However, the University's concession on the agency shop produced what one observer described as a "firestorm" of protest from managers, particularly those in the campus medical school, and from the anti-union C&Ts who felt betrayed by the administration. Some union negotiators believed this reaction made the University afraid to compromise further.

The following day, a fifteen-hour bargaining session produced an agreement on promotions and transfers. Yale agreed to give preference to current employees applying for promotion or transfer in competition with an external applicant unless the latter was "significantly" more qualified. At an 11 P.M. caucus, union negotiators agreed that sufficient progress was being made in negotiations to justify postponing the strike deadline by 24 hours.

A marathon bargaining session on March 28 resulted in a minor concession from Yale on promotions and transfers. While pro-union students camped in sleeping bags in the hallway outside the negotiating room, the two sides attempted to resolve remaining issues. When the session finally adjourned at 1:30 A.M., the union announced a postponement of the strike deadline to April 4. However, the extra five days saw only a few minor procedural issues resolved and a slight increase in Yale's financial offer.

On April 4, with no realistic hope left of resolving the outstanding issues before the strike deadline, Wilhelm proposed to the union negotiating team a novel solution: an interim settlement, or "partial contract," that would codify all language agreed upon up to that point. He argued that if Local 34 went out on strike, the University would not be bound to honor any of the agreements made in the previous months. Wilhelm warned that the timing for a strike was inauspicious. When summer vacation arrived in a few weeks, many areas of the campus would essentially shut down, diluting the impact of a walkout. If the union signed the "partial contract," bargaining on unresolved issues (chiefly wages, benefits, and job security) could continue and the union would retain its right to strike at a later date without jeopardizing the gains already attained. Having made his case, Wilhelm disclosed that New Haven's Congressional representative Bruce Morrison had offered to take the suggestion of the partial contract to the University negotiators to ease its adoption. After considerable debate within their ranks, the Local 34 negotiating team endorsed Wilhelm's plan and agreed to recommend it unanimously to a membership meeting already called for that afternoon.

Such a recommendation was the last thing that the clerical and technical workers had expected when they crowded into Yale's Payne-Whitney gymnasium. As Local 34 members awaited the Negotiating Committee's appearance, the atmosphere of the gym was charged with anticipation. After months of mounting frustration, the C&Ts were prepared, some even eager, to walk picket lines the following morning. When the Local 34 Negotiating Committee entered the gym, a raucous ovation broke out. As the applause subsided, a nervous Wilhelm stepped to the microphone and, in a prepared statement, presented the interim settlement proposal. At that point, as Andrea Ross recalled, "All hell broke loose." After Wilhelm spoke, members of the Negotiating Committee had to field a barrage of hostile questions. Beverly Lett remembers feeling "like I was wearing a big target and people were going to shoot me."

Many in the audience cried and some stalked out believing that they had been betrayed by the negotiating team. After more than three hours of debate, the membership ratified the partial contract by a secret ballot vote of 906-353. That so many voted for a scheme that hours earlier was inconceivable was due both to the credibility the negotiating team had among the members and to the obvious difficulty of sustaining morale in a strike that the leadership opposed. As they left the gym, however, some angry union members told television and newspaper reporters that they were disgusted that the partial contract left economic issues unaddressed. One of these members quipped, "Where's the beef? It's a totally vegetarian contract!"

The dissension over ratification of the partial contract produced the greatest single crisis in the short history of Local 34. However decisive the vote appeared, the mood of the membership was deeply ambivalent—a mixture of relief, disappointment, hope, bitterness, and uncertainty. Ill feelings over the agreement caused some previously active members to stop attending union meetings. Local 34 organizers worked hard that summer to persuade those members that the union had secured important gains by the partial contract, including explicit grievance procedures. In time, the organizers even came to believe that the debate over the partial contract had benefited the union. According to Andrea Ross:

One of the strengths of Local 34 . . . is that we went through the experience early on of the union being literally torn apart with everybody floundering in every direction and we had to go out there and literally pull the union back up by its bootstraps.

The University had less trouble than the union did accepting the idea of a partial contract. Union organizer Warren Heyman reported that the administration bargainers not only seemed to like the concept of a partial contract, but they "proposed it as *their* idea and even sweetened the pie a little bit by saying that all future negotiations would take place on campus and that the Negotiating Committee would be paid for their lost [work] time." In addition, the University agreed under the partial contract to recognize the right of Local 34 members to honor the picket lines of any Local 35 strike.

It is impossible to know precisely why the University, at this stage in negotiations, finally made some significant concessions and agreed to the partial contract. Some observers suggested that Yale had come to recognize that Local 34 was prepared for a strike, and that the blue-collar workers would honor the picket lines. Others theorized that Yale officials had hoped that once the administration accepted the partial contract, "union management" would be so grateful for Local 34's recognition that they would not push hard on the economic issues.

Despite high hopes for a quick settlement of remaining issues, union and University bargainers made little further progress over the remainder of April. Yale increased its total salary offer by only .4% over its previous offer. Moreover, it did not address the structural problems which kept most employees near the bottom of the salary range. The only significant increase in fringe benefits was a dental plan which covered only the employee (not the family), would not start for over two years, and provided only limited coverage. Union members jokingly dubbed it the "one-tooth plan."

With most of the non-economic questions settled by the partial contract, the union shifted its focus to the issue of salary discrimination. In early May, Wilhelm proposed that the University and the union create a committee to gather information about the salary distribution by sex and race in the clerical and technical ranks. The University rejected the need for such a fact-finding committee and proposed that an already agreed upon joint University-union Committee on Job Descriptions and Classification later explore charges of "an inappropriate classification structure."

The union responded with a leaflet containing its own analysis of the University's salary figures, contending that they revealed that "female C&Ts earn less than males, even though the women have worked at Yale longer." Local 34 similarly asserted that "black employees earn less than white employees, even though blacks have worked at Yale longer." The union suggested that the University's refusal even to investigate such evidence ran counter to its image as an institution devoted to principles of equality and the pursuit of truth.

If the concept of pay equity was now more prominent in the union's rhetoric, it had not fallen from the sky. Many clerical and technical workers had been drawn to the union because they believed they were treated unfairly by Yale because they were women. This sentiment was expressed by Deborah Chernoff who disliked the University's attempt to force her into the role of "office-wife or office-mother" and had regarded the union as a means of "standing up for the right's of women, women empowering themselves, not being controlled or dominated by the male hierarchy at Yale." Similarly Lucille Dickess, a C&T in the Yale Geology Department, observed that many women joined the union because they felt the value of their work was ignored by the University: "So many times, female administrative assistants run entire departments, and yet you have got this peacock of a chairman strutting around as if *he* has done all of this, as if *he* is responsible for all of this." The resentment of some female C&Ts against mistreatment by Yale had taken considerable time to surface. Pearl Moore, secretary of the Slavic Department, described herself as having been "very unquestioning about being exploited" during most of her fourteen years at Yale. But the union, Moore reported, had convinced her "that women have a lot of power and can make their lives better." Frequent expressions of such feminist sentiments by Local 34 members appealed to campus women's organizations which, in turn, provided the union with consistent support.

Drawing upon this feminist sensibility, Local 34 organized a one-day strike for May 23 terming it "59-Cent Day." Through this phrase the union sought to call attention to the fact, emphasized by advocates of comparable worth, that the average working woman nationally earned only fifty-nine cents for every dollar earned by a man. At this rally, women carried placards that superimposed upon Yale's pale blue "Y," a jet black 59ᶜ with a slash through it. In addition to its symbolic significance the one-day walkout, according to Deborah Chernoff, was intended to "demonstrate the possibility of having a real strike at Yale," to "prove that people were willing to go without pay to show their discontent with University salary policies."

Despite these varied efforts by Local 34 to bring pressure to bear upon the administration, the end of the school year brought no sign that a final settlement could be reached. At the University graduation in late May, the union held a mass demonstration, forcing the procession of administrators, faculty, and graduating students to march through a gauntlet of sign-carrying Local 34 members and their supporters. Many of the graduates wore green ribbons as pro-union insignia during the ceremonies, which ironically included the presentation of an honorary degree to civil rights and union activist Bayard Rustin. With the departure of the students for summer vacation, the union members realized that they would have to wait until the beginning of the fall semester before a strike could seriously threaten University life.

In late June, the administration stunned many C&Ts by announcing that Yale would not give its traditional July 1 pay raise because the contract with Local 34 remained unsettled. A letter sent by the administration to the clerical and technical workers cited as the reason for the University's inability to implement the normal schedule of salary increases the union's failure to "come forth with any reasonable response to the University's offer." Outraged at what they saw as a petty decision, over 350 union members demonstrated in front of the Yale personnel office.

During the summer, Local 34 persisted in its efforts to make the progress of negotiations as public an issue as possible. At the union's urging, approximately 100 faculty members signed requests to be allowed to observe the negotiations, a proposal the administration quickly rejected. Local 34 responded by allowing professors to join its negotiating team as observers. Moreover, as during the NLRB hearings, the union found it beneficial to bring groups of C&Ts to the bargaining sessions as observers. Steve Fortes recalls that C&Ts who had thought that his description of Yale's high-handed negotiating style were exaggerated left those meetings convinced that indeed Yale was negotiating in bad faith.

September brought students back to campus; it also brought back discussion among the C&Ts of a strike at Yale. On September 13, union members voted by a ten-to-one margin to walk off their jobs in thirteen days if all outstanding issues were not settled.

As in the preceding spring, the union and its supporters arranged a variety of activities to generate campus and community pressure upon the University to improve its offer. The largest of these events, held on September 21, was a rally in front of the building where the Yale Corporation was holding its regular monthly meeting. More than 1,800 people, carrying placards and balloons and singing folk songs, gathered to hear various speakers. Bayard Rustin, his honorary degree from Yale only four months old, spoke, as did representatives from the National Organization for Women, and faculty and student support groups. Rustin drew loud applause when he endorsed Local 34's demands and declared: "I would not work under circumstances when I did not have equal pay, for myself, and for others." The rally culminated in a skit performed by members of Local 34 parodying the meeting of the Yale Corporation. Wendy Wipprecht, the C&T who portrayed President Giamatti, recalled, "There was something about laughing at the Corporation members, who were really out to cut our throats, that was profoundly liberating."

As the strike deadline approached, many students and faculty members expressed their concern that the University was not seriously considering the impact a strike would have on campus life. New petitions addressed to the Yale Corporation urging the submission of outstanding issues to arbitration were signed by over 2,000 students and 150 Yale faculty. In addition to these demonstrations of campus support, thirteen state legislators from the New Haven area signed a public letter also endorsing binding arbitration.

The union's September 21-22 efforts to persuade the Yale Corporation of the need for binding arbitration ultimately failed. After the Corporation's two-day meeting J. Richardson Dilworth, one of its prominent members, addressed the point in a letter to John Wilhelm, declaring "that binding arbitration is unacceptable, now or at any time in the future, as a means to settling the remaining terms of this contract . . . ." On September 23, the union significantly reduced its salary demands. The administration replied that it could only "rearrange the furniture," but not increase the total value of its package. Two days later, Yale announced that it had made its "final offer" to the union.

While some progress had been made since the signing of the partial contract in April, the two sides still remained far apart on economic issues. The difference in the costs of the two side's proposals averaged over $4 million for each year of the contract, the largest difference lying in the across-the-board increases: the University offered 6.5%, 5.3%, and 5.3% in the three years of the contract while the union asked for 9%, 10%, and 10%. The union also wanted a cost-of-living adjustment set at three-quarters of inflation while the University offered no inflation adjustment. Over the summer, the University had finally accepted the principle of annual "step" increases but had not yet agreed with the union on the amount of such increases. A large gap also remained on the issue of pensions. The administration adamantly opposed the union's demand that Yale increase its contribution to the pension fund from 8% of salaries to roughly 10%, a percentage that the University already contributed to its faculty's plan.

Union negotiators rejected the University's "final offer," and agreed among themselves that no realistic hope remained to avert a strike. Rather than bargain fruitlessly through the night, the Local 34 team broke off negotiations early in the evening of September 25 and announced that a strike would begin at 5 A.M. the next day. As they watched the 11 P.M. news reports, Local 34 members and the entire Yale community learned that a strike would occur the next morning.

Supporting a Strike

The appearance of picket lines at buildings across the Yale campus on September 26, 1984, marked the beginning of an event that would turn that prestigious university into the scene of one of the more dramatic labor disputes in recent times. Over the next ten weeks, academic life at Yale would be all but eclipsed by the battle between Local 34 and the administration. In the meantime, the strike would draw close attention around the country to the issues it raised, the workers it involved, and the strategies it developed.

Approximately 1,700 workers—nearly two-thirds of the University's secretaries, telephone operators, library workers, computer programmers, research assistants, laboratory technicians, and hospital aides—stayed out. Most could be found on one of the scores of picket lines that dotted the campus. These lines were honored by roughly 95 percent of Yale's maintenance and service workers, no strangers to strikes themselves. The impact of their absence on the functioning of the university was felt immediately. Twelve of the thirteen campus dining halls were closed, depriving students in the Residential Colleges not only of their meals, but of their primary meeting spots as well. With refunds on their unfilled meal contracts in hand, students scoured neighborhood restaurants and grocery stores for food. They also found themselves looking for their classes, well over 100 of which had been moved to off-campus locations by professors and instructors who sympathized with the strikers (approximately 400 more waited for new spaces to become available). Classes met in such unlikely settings as church halls, public libraries, movie theaters, union offices, restaurants, and dozens of private homes around the Yale area. University libraries, woefully understaffed, curtailed their hours. In many offices, telephones went unanswered and letters untyped. Meanwhile, college residences were not cleaned, with results that would become increasingly difficult to ignore as the strike wore on.

Other consequences of the strike sank in more gradually. University fundraising efforts lost much of their efficiency and appeal; attention to the physical plant declined; research goals were postponed; performances, speaking engagements, and conferences were canceled; and the activities of the great array of extracurricular societies were interrupted.

The impact of the strike on the psychological atmosphere of Yale was even more significant. The diverse collection of workers who made up Local 34 had done more than withdraw their labor; their presence as strikers transformed the campus into a moral battleground that engulfed all parts of the Yale community. In the opening days of the strike, even those parts of academic life that continued were overshadowed by the drama unfolding on the streets. Students, faculty, non-striking employees, and visitors were all called upon to decide which side they were on. At every turn they encountered picket lines, urging them—through literature, chants, and one-on-one persuasion—not to follow "business as usual" so long as the strike continued. A union leaflet distributed throughout the Yale community at the outset of the strike spelled out what this meant:

We recognize that certain activities may be difficult to avoid, such as sleeping in your campus room or attending classes that aren't moved off campus.

Beyond those things that are absolutely unavoidable, we ask that you ensure that "business as usual" will not prevail at Yale while we are forced to be on strike. Some examples are:

1. We ask that no voluntary events, such as parties, conferences, speeches, etc., be held on campus. . . .

2. We ask that you use no Yale facilities (the libraries, the gym, dining halls, etc.).

3. If you must use those facilities which are absolutely essential to your educational duties (the library, computer center, classrooms, [and] laboratories), we ask that you protest directly to the Yale administration each time you must do so.

4. We ask that you attend no Yale events. It is critical that the administration not be permitted to maintain Yale's national reputation as a center of intellectual activity while it is forcing us to strike for our dignity.

5. We also ask that your classes, groups, and organizations periodically interrupt their activities to join us on the picket line, and to make your views known to the administration.

As members of the Yale community responded in various ways to this call, the center of gravity on campus shifted from the classrooms, libraries, and laboratories to the streets. At the core of this activity were the picket lines, daily reminders that Yale was not in a state of normalcy. Their presence flooded the senses, with the sight of workers carrying signs reading "On Strike for Respect"; with the unrelieved din of chanting and singing, and cars honking their support; and with the overall tension that these lines brought to the surface.

The picket lines served as rallying point for strikers and their supporters. It was on the lines where many strikers learned the latest information from their picket captains, where money was raised, where strategies were debated, and where strikers' morale was bolstered. It was also on the lines that the moods of the strikers found their widest range of expression, from anger to celebration, nervousness, giddiness, weariness, or frustration. There were also rallies and press conferences, letters and phone calls, meetings and fund-raising events, informal gatherings of strikers and countless debates, large and small, but as the focus of the confrontation, the picket lines were the single most important mechanism in the strike.

From the outset it was clear that the strike could not be won in the traditional manner—that is, by completely closing down the workplace. That would have required not only the involvement of a greater number of C&Ts, roughly one-third of whom remained on the job, but also a broad willingness among students and teachers to interrupt their scholarly pursuits in order to support the strike. Local 34's decision not to call for total cessation of academic activity was, above all, a pragmatic one: first, it sought to avoid appearing indifferent to the mission of the University; and second, it was reluctant to call for a type of support that it knew it could not get. However realistic, this stance posed a perplexing issue for union sympathizers who had always believed that a picket line was inviolable. Some supporters could not bring themselves to cross under any circumstances. But others felt it necessary, thus joining the many more who, indifferent or hostile to the union, felt no dilemma at all.

Adding to the difficulty of winning the strike in the standard fashion was the decentralized layout of Yale's workplace. With offices dispersed throughout the campus, the University could function, or at least hobble along, with only a minority of its total work force. Overall the strike could reduce the quality and pace of work dramatically, and it could shatter the serenity of University life, but it could not close the place down in the manner of a strike at a coal mine or an auto plant. Moreover, what effect the strike was having on the operations of the University was difficult to gauge. Rather than consumer products, Yale engages in the production of knowledge; whatever impact the strike had on such an intangible could not easily be established. Furthermore, much of the strike's effect was cumulative, becoming evident only with the passage of time.

However, Yale was quite vulnerable on another front—that of its image to the outside world. Here, after all, was its true capital. What ultimately makes Yale succeed is less its levels of productivity or profit than its aura of enlightenment, integrity, and moral leadership. Such a reputation is crucial to its continued material and intellectual wealth. But no matter how carefully cultivated, Yale's mystique could not long withstand the glare of national attention that the strike had attracted. For millions of Americans (and thousands of alumni), the image of Yale as a haven of higher intellectual purpose gave place to a series of more down-to-earth pictures: speeches, chants, and picket signs charged the administration with union-busting, discrimination, stinginess, and dishonesty; students and faculty complained of a chaotic, polarized campus; mass acts of civil disobedience dramatized the strikers' conviction that they were engaged in a struggle for social justice; and images of these activities were conveyed through the coverage of newspapers, magazines, network news programs, even the Phil Donahue Show. Those unmoved by the moral implications for the University might still be disturbed by the impact of the dispute on the physical state of the campus. A description in the *Los Angeles Times* typified what the media wrote, and the cameras showed:

Since September 26, about 400 classes have been moved to chilly church basements, dimly-lit movie theatres, crowded living rooms, and packed pizza parlors. Twelve of 13 student dining rooms are closed. Laboratories are curtailed; the law school is deserted. Bags of garbage piled in halls, dormitory bathrooms remain uncleaned, and litter lines the neat Old Campus. Police on horseback patrol near the massive Gothic buildings.

Business Week noted the arrival of cockroaches in the dormitories; the *Wall Street Journal* found Yale "a crippled university."

Acutely conscious of the importance of solidarity and public opinion, the union invested a great deal of energy in mobilizing the support of students, faculty, other Yale workers, the New Haven community, and key figures and organizations around the country. The critical source of assistance continued to be the maintenance and service workers of Local 35. In addition to the loss of their services, the refusal of blue-collar workers to cross picket lines meant a powerful infusion of moral support from a group of workers whose own campaigns had opened the door for the creation of Local 34. As the days and weeks passed, practically no one in Local 35 returned. Not amused, the administration launched a formal grievance against Local 35 charging its leaders with breach of contract by encouraging its members to walk out in sympathy with Local 34. To make the pressure more immediate, the administration sent a personal letter to each member of Local 35 threatening disciplinary action against those who failed to come to work. Such tactics backfired. On the evening of October 2, five hundred members of Local 35 assembled at the Methodist Church and marched to President Giamatti's house, where each deposited into a box (gamely held out by Yale police officers) a small blue card reading, "I'm out. I have a right to be out.

I'm staying out. Yale should settle or arbitrate.''

The support of Local 35 members for Local 34 provided the uncommon sight of blue- and white-collar employees joining forces in a labor struggle. The willingness of the maintenance and service workers to forfeit their pay in a difficult battle for someone else's contract was all the more remarkable in light of the indifference clerical and technical workers had shown, in the days before their own organizing drive, to the strikes of Local 35. However, in the intervening years, the growth and tenacity of the office and laboratory workers had impressed their blue-collar colleagues. Mike Santarcangelo, a Yale powerhouse engineer for 21 years, captured that feeling: ''You've got to love these women—they're very gutsy people.'' But more than admiration, blue-collar support for Local 34 sprang from a sense of mutual interest. As Local 35 member Robert West said, ''If Yale finds it can take down one union, it's going to take down all of them.'' No one in Local 35 needed to be reminded that their own contract was due to expire in a few months. Added another Local 35 member, ''It's either walk with the pickets now or walk them in the winter.''

The alliance not only strengthened the hand of each union; it also had an important impact on their respective outlooks. The clerical and technical workers, most of whom had little if any grounding in the way of unions and strikes, drew experience and confidence from the veterans of Local 35, whereas the blue-collar workers, for their part, became sensitized to the issue of sex discrimination at the workplace. It was this shared sense of revelation, as well as collective power, that gave the strike much of its dramatic edge.

Also figuring prominently in the outcome of the strike was the student body. By the time the strike began, a network of student support groups was already well in place. Mobilization of sympathetic undergraduates was carried out by Students for a Negotiated Settlement; a parallel function was performed by the Graduate and Professional Students Support Group. Operating out of a room at Yale's Dwight Chapel, these groups devised a wide range of strategies to organize student support and keep the pressure on the University to settle. Top priorities included persuading students to honor—better yet, to walk—the picket lines, to write or call Yale administrators urging a just settlement, to convince their parents (many of them alumni) to do likewise, to ask their teachers to move their classes off-campus, to attend rallies, to donate portions of their dining-hall rebates to the strike fund, to induce extracurricular organizations to endorse the strike, and to raise the issue of the strike in class, at dinner, in passing conversation. The response of students was so critical because education lay at the heart of Yale's mission, and it was a mission with which most strikers identified. Even those who detested the administration could feel genuine regret over the disruption the strike brought to the students' lives. A show of support from students could provide a powerful emotional boost. The attitudes of the students also had a tactical importance: for better or worse, the media tended to focus more on their ordeal during the strike than on that of the strikers.

Undeniably meaningful, student reactions were also varied, ambivalent, often confused, and always in flux. The responses and debates were particularly intense among the undergraduates, who were most deeply immersed in campus life, and hence most vulnerable to the impact of the strike. Not many of them came from union backgrounds; most, indeed, came out of homes that ranged from upper middle-class to wealthy. Few had ever encountered a strike that affected them so directly. Jolted from the self-enclosed pursuits of college life into the midst of a bitter, real-life conflict, every student was confronted with the need to learn quickly the issues and formulate some opinions and principles to guide his or her actions. No one could escape the clamor so evident in the opinion section of the *Yale Daily News*, in the crossfire of propaganda issued by the union and the administration, in the debates that dominated discussions on the streets and in classrooms and restaurants, and above all in the picket lines that greeted students at every turn.

Many students lost little time demonstrating their opposition to the union and to unions generally. Some went out of their way to express their views. One student, while passing briskly through a picket line, muttered, "I'm paying $15,000 to go to Yale!" Another found a less articulate, but more dramatic way to show his resentment: passing through the picket line at Bienecke Plaza, he made a point of kicking over the strikers' donuts and coffee. Anti-union sentiment even worked its way into verse, exemplified by one hand-written effort—mocking the union chant, "We are Local 34!"—sighted on the wall of the Yale campus post office:

> *One, two, three, four,*
> *Who is Local 34?*
> *Five, six, seven, eight,*
> *They claim Yale discriminates!*
>
> *One, two, three, four,*
> *They won't work, they want more!*
> *Five, six, seven, eight,*
> *Bart, push them out, lock the gates!*

More common than such extreme hostility among students were intermingled feelings of confusion, indifference, and resentment over being drawn into a battle that they did not consider their problem. For many, the classic labor refrain that during a strike "there are no neutrals" rang no bells. "It's a dispute between the administration and the C&Ts," said one junior. "Attempts to disrupt academic life are wrong. We really don't have much to do with it." Another student viewed as a provocation the union's assertion that everyone must take a stand: "It's obvious that the idea is to use the students."

Some students expressed a measure of sympathy for the workers, but explained that their work came first. One allowed, "A lot of [freshmen] like the idea of the union—that theoretically an injustice can be remedied by group participation. That's nice in the history book." But not when it disrupts classes, she added. A junior, in a letter to the *Yale Daily News*, was more candid: "My concern in this issue is primarily selfish, I admit. All I want is to go back to my classes, eat my meals in my dining hall, and return to the normally comfortable life of a Yale undergrad as soon as possible." But many of those who chose these priorities still experienced stress engendered by the conflict. This effect was poignantly illustrated by a student interviewed by the *Yale Daily News:*

It can be a source of conflict to cross the picket lines. I used to work

in a Kline Biology Tower lab. Two technicians I'd worked with were
standing in the picket line. My first instinct was to say hi, but I real-
ized I had crossed their picket line by going to class. So I did not
greet them.

A vocal minority of students rallied to the side of the union. For
those raised in union (or at least pro-union) families, the decision
came rather easily. For others, recruitment to the cause was a trans-
forming experience. ''I got involved,'' said one student, ''because
I believed Yale was forsaking its ideals and these workers were being
paid unjustly. People are tired of being labeled the apathetic genera-
tion. There is a sense that we are reclaiming something. I don't know
what you call it—a sense of honesty, principles, ideals.'' A senior
told the *Los Angeles Times*, ''I think maybe the strike is more important than my senior thesis.'' One junior saw a link between her
academic life and her stand on the strike: ''In respecting the right
of Yale's employees to protest the conditions of their employment,
I use my intellectual capacities as a basis for a real moral choice.''

Some students felt a bond with the crusade of Local 34 as women
or minorities. Bernice Houseman, a senior, wrote, ''Women at all
levels of the University structure are chronically underpaid, over-
worked, and not given the recognition they deserve. I challenge all
women students at Yale to ask themselves . . . where do you think
you will be when you graduate: can you guarantee you won't be
picketing for the same rights?'' This question had special credibility
in light of the fact that a number of Local 34 members were Yale
graduates. Similarly, two Asian students, Dorothy Rony and Monica
Yin, identified as minorities with the union cause. In a letter to the
campus paper they wrote: ''The closed and defensive stance which
the Corporation, et al., have taken towards Local 34's grievances
matches the administration's unwillingness to act on minority
students' needs. . . . Whether on the student or employee level, we
are striving for the same dignity and equality.'' Women's and
minorities' groups in support of Local 34 were active during the
strike.

Pro-union students found a number of ways to express support for

Local 34. These included such high-profile activities as rallies, sit-ins, petition drives, fund-raising activities, picket lines around campus sports and cultural events, a teach-in for the Yale community on the issues of the strike (organized jointly with pro-union faculty), and press conferences. Student initiatives which gained particularly wide attention were a campaign to withhold tuition payment for the spring semester and a lawsuit brought by 102 students against the university for breach of contract (because of disruption of services due to the strike). In addition to these organized efforts, there were many individual touches, such as the appearance of several Yale cheerleaders at the football games with the words "Yale Settle" sewn onto their sweaters, bed sheets hanging from the windows of college residence halls bearing messages of support for the union, and a mischievous offer by students in the School of Organization and Management to give President Giamatti "a refresher course in management practices," together with a "remedial" reading list containing such essential literature as *Megatrends* and *In Search of Excellence*.

Because the words of Yale professors commanded respect, they too became the target of ongoing appeals from both the union and the University. As with the student body, the faculty spanned a wide spectrum of opinion regarding the strike. Some held that the administration's offer was already too generous. Economist William Nordhaus, for instance, lamented that "[a] settlement that high [as the proposal] will impose pain on all who teach, work and learn here." Others had a very different perspective. John Trinkaus, a professor of biology in his thirty-sixth year on the Yale faculty, asked, "Is the University a corporation that makes ball-bearings, or is it a company of scholars [who can make responsible decisions]. . . ? A great many of us love it here. I want to be proud of Yale, not ashamed of it."

Faculty backing for the union, coordinated by the Faculty Support Group, was expressed most broadly by the removal of classes to off-campus locations. Pro-union faculty also marched in special picket lines outside of Woodbridge Hall where Giamatti worked, published signed ads in the local press, and raised the issue of the strike in the meetings of the Yale College Faculty. On November 1, the most heavily attended meeting of the Yale College Faculty since the height of the Vietnam War convened to consider a resolution calling on the administration to agree to outside binding arbitration. Although the resolution failed, the narrow margin of defeat (164-145) indicated how polarized the faculty had become over the stance of the administration.

No university can thrive without supportive alumni, and private schools are especially reliant upon their goodwill and their money. Naturally, Local 34 and its supporters were eager to win them over. A group of sympathetic alumni coordinated an effort to urge Yale graduates around the country to withhold support from the University, and register their protest over the administration's position in the dispute. One petition directed to President Giamatti and the members of the Yale Corporation and circulated nationally ended thus:

We are deeply dismayed by Yale's intransigence. Not only does it betray the University's humanistic ideals, it reveals a narrow understanding of the Yale "community." As a sign that our commitment to these ideals and to a broader vision of that community, we have chosen not to contribute to the Yale Alumni Fund this year. Instead we are directing our donations to Local 34's strike fund.

The administration meanwhile sent out a number of mailings assuring the alumni of the University's sincerity and integrity during the controversy. In light of their social position, it is likely that most Yale alumni were indifferent if not hostile to the union's cause. Nonetheless, many were likely to have been troubled by the administration's inability to keep the peace at their alma mater, and a good number no doubt chose to direct their financial contributions elsewhere that year.

Local 34 drew ample support from the New Haven community as well. This was hardly surprising given the stark contrast between the wealth of Yale and the poverty of the town. Resentment in New Haven over that contrast was sharpened by Yale's long-standing failure to pay any local taxes. It was intensified still further by the fact that numerous Yale employees were from New Haven, and large numbers of New Haven residents had friends or kin who worked at the University. Widespread antipathy towards Yale or enthusiasm for the union turned up in a number of ways. Local teenagers were reported breakdancing to the union slogan, "Beep, Beep—Yale's Cheap." When Giamatti appeared at a restaurant near campus for lunch, the waitress declined to serve him. "They [Yale] own half of New Haven," said one merchant, "and for the people of New Haven they don't do anything." Local 34 received widespread assistance from community groups and leaders. Local labor, including the Greater New Haven Central Labor Council, the Connecticut AFL-CIO, and the Teamsters, gave financial and political support. The New Haven Board of Aldermen voted 19 to 2 to urge Yale to agree to arbitration, fact-finding, or some other form of compromise. After much deliberation and discussion with each side, the New Haven Black Ministerial Alliance came out for Local 34. The New Haven Board of Rabbis, while maintaining official neutrality, was, like the ministers, instrumental in alleviating the plight of the strikers. For example, they intervened regularly with landlords, asking, often successfully, that delinquency on rent payments be overlooked for the duration of the strike.

Nationwide attention to the strike brought nationwide support. One major source of support was organized labor. Union locals across the country sent financial contributions. AFL-CIO President Lane Kirkland, addressing a Local 34 rally on the New Haven Green, assured an estimated crowd of 1,000 that "Your success will be felt far beyond this University—in workplaces across the land." The racial dimension of the union's fight drew the concern of civil rights leaders as well. And, because of the composition and demands of Local 34, the strike was warmly embraced by the women's movement. Eleanor Smeal, former president of the National Organization for Women, brought to the strikers the message that "people throughout the country are aware of your strike. . . . We are living in a reactionary time. . . . You are walking for people around the country and you are walking for justice." Judy Goldsmith, her successor, also came to Yale to announce the formation of a national committee composed of feminist leaders, to support the strikers.

The broad support of labor, minority, and women's groups rein-forced the sense among the strikers and their supporters of being engaged in a crusade of historical significance. However, that feel-ing was not inspired solely by outsiders. It was rooted in the themes that were sounded and the tactics used by the strikers themselves. Because this aura of a social cause was so essential to the strike, it is worth discussing in depth.

This spirit had several important elements. It drew upon the abili-ty of the union to strip away the mystique of Yale, and reveal in its place the hypocrisy of the University's claims to untainted reason and integrity. Attempts to expose the gulf between the promises and the practice of the University were a regular feature of Local 34's propaganda. The serial Local 34 report to the public on negotiations, *"In Good Faith,"* made the point in the masthead of each issue simply by reprinting Giamatti's statement that had followed the union cer-tification election: "It is now time for us to put aside our differences and in good faith to work together." Yale's failure to live up to its moral purpose was also underscored by frequent reference to the ill-chosen words of another administrator, Provost William Brainard: "I know that one can't live the way one would like to, or the way one would like one's family to, on a Yale clerical and technical worker's salary. That's a national problem, which Yale can't be ex-pected to solve." Other union literature provided thumbnail sketches on each of the trustees. "The members of the Yale Corporation," it explained, "are making the decisions which prolong Local 34's strike. . . . Most people do not know who they are, and so they have largely been able until now to prolong the strike anonymously, without accountability."

But the union and its supporters went beyond claiming that the administration had abdicated its moral leadership of the University; they argued further that the C&Ts' campaign had come to embody the very values that the administration was betraying. "It's the workers who are standing up for *Lux et Veritas,*" sang picketers, to the tune of *Solidarity Forever.* While such lines made effective prop-aganda, they also meant something quite real to the strikers. Rosamund Hamlin recalls, "I was striking for human rights, to be treated with dignity and respect, and to be treated as an individual for the worth of the work that I did . . . so people could retire with dignity, with a decent pension. . .to me, the money was of minor importance; relatively speaking, it was a much smaller issue to me than the issue of individual worth."

The feeling of collective power and purpose that this spirit generated was reinforced by the many ways that strikers found to express themselves. One could scarcely walk through campus without hearing snatches of singing from various picket lines along the way. Old labor standards such as *Union Maids*, *We're Gonna Roll*, and *Ain't Gonna Let Nobody Turn Me Around*, reminded strikers of their place in a historical tradition. In addition to these, new twists cropped up constantly (collected finally into the *Local 34 Songbook*), including adaptations such as *Do Negotiations* (to the tune of *Locomotion*), *Bart (Mame)*, *We're Not At Work Today (Ta Rah Rah Boom De Yay)*, *What's Yale Got To Do With It? (What's Love Got To Do With It?)*, *Giamatti, Look and See (Mr. Postman)*, *Arbitration, Binding Arbitration (Alhouette)*, *We Love You, 35 (We Love You, Conrad)*, and, inevitably, *Bartbusters!* Such tunes not only helped strikers keep their sense of humor through hard times, but they also deepened their sense of community, creativity, and irreverence toward an administration that was fast losing its ability to cow them.

Another source of collective self-confidence was the *Strike Bulletin*, a newsletter written by and for strikers. The nine issues that appeared during October and November kept strikers posted on negotiations and media attention, rallies and fundraising events, activities on the picket lines, and the latest expression of support (or opposition) from within or beyond the Yale community. The first edition, for instance, listed eighteen campus events that had been moved or canceled to honor the picket lines, including a Sierra Club speech by New Haven Congressional representative Bruce Morrison, a talk by actor Ken Howard, a concert by Holly Near and Ronnie Gilbert, a Yale Chinese student "Lunch Table," and a fundraising viewing by the Yale Democrats of the Reagan-Mondale and Ferraro-Bush debates.

A series of demonstrations that spanned the strike further nurtured the belief that victory was possible. These took a number of forms. Noontime rallies brought strikers from all parts of the campus together. Several of these were conducted in silence, as "vigils." Others targeted particular Yale events or figures. A graduate school alumni reception drew 300 pickets. In early October, approximately fifty children of strikers assembled at Woodbridge Hall to submit letters to Giamatti urging a settlement. A number of rallies conducted around the country by HERE locals and support groups at public engagements of the Yale Corporation members, such as Eleanor Holmes Norton, Bishop Paul Moore, and Deborah Rhode—brought attention to the gap between their reputations for liberalism and their failure to speak out for the union's cause.

Most stirring of all were two acts of mass civil disobedience staged by the union during October. On the morning of October 5, one hundred and ninety two union members filed silently from the United Methodist Church to Hillhouse Avenue, stopping in the street in front of President Giamatti's house. There, flanked on both sidewalks by close to a thousand fellow workers and supporters, they submitted one by one to arrest for obstructing traffic. A public statement issued by the union powerfully conveyed the purpose and the mood of the event:

The membership of Local 34 has voted, by secret ballot, to join together in a Nonviolent Witness for Equality at the house of Yale President A. Bartlett Giamatti. As part of that Nonviolent Witness, some of us will submit to peaceful arrest, symbolic of our commitment, in the tradition of Gandhi and Martin Luther King.

We have joined in this Witness because Yale's announced intention to starve us into abandoning our 4-year struggle for equality leaves us no honorable alternative. . . .

We believe that we have been patient beyond any reasonable call. We have negotiated in 73 meetings over a full year, and continue to seek further negotiation. We have compromised. We repeatedly postponed our strike deadlines. We proposed arbitration. We have even agreed not to seek full equality now, but merely to seek a commitment to equality in the future, and a significant down-payment now.

Yale has responded to our patience by massive distortion of our position, and of its own. When we suggested open discussion and debate about these misrepresentations, Yale responded by refusing even to appear in the same room with us. The University has knowingly concealed and distorted the statistical evidence supporting our discrimination charges. It has cynically made secret decisions to use the increased earnings of our pension fund to reduce Yale's level of pension contribution, instead of increasing at no additional cost the pitiful benefits which consign many of us to an old age of poverty.

We are mindful, too, that Yale University has no constructive approach to labor relations, beyond using its great wealth and power to try to dictate a contract. No other Connecticut employer, and probably no other American employer, has had five strikes during the last 16 years at one location, involving two entirely different groups of employees.

We are, finally, painfully aware of the campaign of threats and harassment Yale has directed against our brothers and sisters in Local 35 because they have felt compelled not to cross a picket line made up of their wives, daughters, friends, neighbors and co-workers.

Yale has told us, and the community, that it will never bend or compromise, but will merely wait until we—and our children—starve.

That is not what has made Yale a great university. It is against this denial of Yale's own values that we witness.

This spirit of indignation and high purpose was everywhere in evidence during the witness. Each arrestee wore a sign reading, "*Lux et Veritas?*" Individual signs added other points. Read one: "There are no criminals here: we are good workers whom Yale wants to break." And another: "What if I were your mother?" "I've never been arrested before," one participant told the campus paper. "But we're making a statement, very simply, that the Giamatti administration no longer stands for any real world ideals."

As such statements indicate, willfully breaking the law was not a casual thing for most of the arrestees. The very decision to bill the event a "nonviolent witness" instead of "civil disobedience" was made to calm the uneasiness that the more familiar term stirred among many members. Warren Heyman, who helped mobilize the event, relates what joining the witness could entail: "I had some phenomenal talks with people who said, 'Last night I had to sit down with my kids and talk to them about why I was going to break the law and get arrested after I'd been telling them for the last ten years, you never break the law; you always do what a police officer says.'" Even a rank-and-file organizer like Steve Fortes recalled feeling "a few reservations" at the prospect of being arrested: "It's very difficult when everyone is brought up with the notion that you don't break the law or that you don't get arrested. There's a stigma attached to it which is really hard to overcome." But it was precisely that internal conflict that lent the mass arrest such emotional power. Even Giamatti had to acknowledge that it was "a sad but dignified event." It strengthened the resolve of the workers at a time when it was becoming increasingly apparent that the strike would not be settled soon, and it provided a compelling image to television viewers around the country.

Three weeks later, on October 26, an even larger witness was held outside Woodbridge Hall, where the Yale Corporation was scheduled to meet. This time 434 people, supporters as well as strikers, formed two long rows down the middle of New Haven's Wall Street, joined by over a thousand supporters along the sidewalks. First to be arrested was Bayard Rustin, who had returned from New York for the event. "I believe," he said, "that having been made a part of the Yale community by receiving an honorary degree, I am here not by choice but because I have a moral obligation. I stand by the workers and against injustices to minorities and women. I believe that whenever people quietly demonstrate—like Martin Luther King, Jr. and Tolstoy and Gandhi—people will listen." No less inspiring was the appearance of King's closest associate throughout the civil rights movement, Reverend Ralph Abernathy, to offer his encouragement to the arrestees as they assembled at the United Methodist Church before the arrest. The gathering fell silent as Abernathy gave his blessing:

I'm a man that stood by Martin Luther King. In my arms Martin Luther King died on the Lorraine Motel balcony in Memphis, Tennessee. . . . Take it from one who's been to jail 44 times and beaten until I thought I was dead. Nothing comes to oppressed people without suffering. Privileged classes do not give up their rights without a struggle. . . . Yale is a great institution. Yale is a wealthy institution. But Yale is treating certain segments of its population unjustly and Yale University ought to be ashamed. . . . You have the opportunity to witness for justice and equality . . . for a grand and noble cause.

"At that point," remembered Fortes, "it really felt like this was something that was truly history."

Such moments of elation, however crucial, were not easy to sustain. As the strike stretched into November and then passed Thanksgiving, the union would be faced with the increasingly difficult task of preserving the morale and resources of its members.

Sticking to the Union

P hil Voigt, chief steward of Local 35 and a veteran of four Yale strikes, reflects: "It's always the first couple of weeks [in a strike] when everybody gets nervous and says 'When are they going to settle? When are we going back to work? I need money, my family needs money,' and so on, then after the second week, everybody gets into the groove and says 'Okay, it's going to take a while'."

Even after the second and third weeks of Local 34's strike, however, no one really knew how long "a while" would be. "Everybody would say the same thing, and we all meant it," said Lucille Dickess, who has worked at Yale for seventeen years and is now Local 34's president: "We'll be out for as long as it takes. . . ." Yet as the strike wore on, and Yale continually refused to alter its "final offer," the walkout became increasingly draining for the women and men on the picket lines. In mid-October, Local 34 strikers, and their supporters in Local 35, began receiving fifty dollars a week picket pay from the Hotel and Restaurant Employee's Union, but this could not cover all the bills. Local 34 relied on a system of support mechanisms—both material and moral—designed to ensure that the members' determination to stay out would not be jeopardized by the mounting stresses of the strike.

Many of Yale's clerical and technical workers who walked the picket lines were new to unionism and had not been through a strike before. In dealing with the financial strains, assistance provided to the workers by the veteran unionists in Local 35 proved invaluable. Workers in Local 35, along with other union members in New Haven, offered advice concerning services already available within the community, like the Fuel Assistance Program. Before the strike began, the union established a Resources Committee to deal with financial problems that the members of Local 34 and Local 35 would encounter. Rosamund Hamlin, an administrative assistant in the Geology Department, served on this committee throughout the strike. "In the initial stages [of the strike]," she recalls, "much of what we did was simply counseling and reassurance. We tried to tell people what they could do to help themselves—in other words, to contact their banks, to contact their creditors if there was going to be a problem."

As the strike continued, the Resources Committee became more directly involved with the financial problems of the strikers. The union sent out letters to local utilities, banks, and insurance companies, requesting that contact persons be assigned in these institutions to deal with strikers' problems. When sympathetic clergymen offered their assistance, the committee had Local 34 poll strikers to determine if they wished to have a minister or rabbi contact their landlord to ask that rent payments be postponed or temporarily reduced.

Members of the committee negotiated with local banks regarding mortgage payments, and in fact drew an assurance from one, the largest mortgage holder in the community, that it would not repossess homes for the duration of the strike. The Resources Committee also attempted to find part-time work for union members, and established a typing service to make use of the skills of striking clericals. Supportive students and faculty paid Local 34 members to type their papers and reports.

"We tried to solve problems without an outlay of funds," says Hamlin. Yet this was not always possible. When cash was necessary, the union could turn to two different sources. The union's own strike fund, used also to finance the day-to-day operations of the walkout, was utilized by the Resources Committee in cases of immediate need. The union also relied on the Hardship Fund, which operated out of the Yale chaplain's office.

The Hardship Fund, originally established during a previous Local 35 walkout, was revived when the Local 34 strike began. Requests for aid from this source were first processed through the union, and then forwarded to an eight-person committee, consisting of several chaplains in addition to members of Local 34, faculty, and students, who determined the amount of money to be given to the individual striker; checks were then sent directly to the landlord or creditor. The independent status of the Hardship Fund gave it particular importance in a University environment. It became easier to solicit donations from those at Yale who sympathized with the strikers' plight but did not wish to make a "pro-union" statement.

The strikers knew that cash was available for them in cases of financial crisis, and yet the funds were not continually being exhausted. "Many of them [the strikers] felt that most of the other people must need more help than they did," says Hamlin. "It was quite extraordinary to me to see the minimal amounts that people asked for, and how long they held back."

Such forbearance was due in part to the help that strikers gave each other. "There was a tremendous strength and spirit and openness on the lines," recalls Hamlin. "If somebody knew that somebody's car was being repossessed, or if a striker had little children and only a quart of milk in the house, money would be collected on the picket lines to help out." Lucille Dickess agrees. "It was a revelation to me the way people truly cared about each other and helped each other during the strike." She notes that fundraising on the lines became particularly important, both to lift spirits and to raise cash:

Yale's clericals and technicals are very inventive and imaginative—you have to be to exist around here on the salaries we get—so of course there were lots of novel ways of making money on the lines. There were bake sales and tag sales—I especially loved the tag sale in front of 155 Whitney [a Yale administration building]. Here the administrators were going in to work and there was this union tag sale in front of them.

There were, of course, more formal ways of raising money. Local 34 had its own fund-raising committee, made up of union members, students, and faculty, as well as representatives from community groups, labor organizations, and the clergy. The committee met once a week throughout the strike. Often members of the committee organized their own activities to bring money into the strike fund: graduate students sponsored a dance; the Central Labor Council held a raffle and used the proceeds to buy Christmas presents for strikers' children. Sales of "59 Cent" buttons, "Bartbuster" t-shirts, and *Local 34 Songbooks* brought in additional money. The committee appealed to local merchants for contributions; some made weekly donations. New Haven and Connecticut unions gave generous financial support and their help proved crucial. Committee members estimated that together all of these activities brought in close to $100,000 by the strike's end.

Many, if not most, of the contributions came in response not to formal solicitations but through word of mouth. New Haven residents walked into the Resources Committee office with checks for ten or twenty dollars to make things easier; the parents of discontented Yale students sent donations to union headquarters. Contributions came in addition from people throughout the country who had no direct connection with Yale, but had read or heard about the clerical and technical workers' struggle and wanted to help them win.

Local 34's campaign to provide the strike with extensive local and national publicity was thus important, and the union utilized news coverage to strengthen its position. At the outset, the walkout drew considerable notice, due in large part to Yale's reputation, to Local 34's emphasis on the comparable worth issue, and to the increasing significance of clerical unionism. However, labor issues rarely receive lasting attention from the national media; the Yale strike would probably have faded from view had Local 34 not developed creative strategies and had the union not remained continually attuned to the importance of press coverage. Publicity attracted financial support; it kept the University on the defensive; and it helped to lift the flagging spirits of the strikers themselves by demonstrating the significance of their effort.

Local 34's attention to the media paid off. Various aspects of the strike were covered by all three national television networks, by newspapers such as the *New York Times*, the *Los Angeles Times*, and the *Wall Street Journal*, by journals as diverse as *Newsweek*, *Radical*

America, *The Nation*, *New England Business*, *The Village Voice*, and *U.S. News and World Report*, and by the MacNeil-Lehrer Newshour and the Phil Donahue Show.

The union recognized that reporters not inclined to cover a "simple" labor dispute might nonetheless be interested in the unusual problems created by a strike in a university setting. Local 34 members and sympathizers led reporters on tours of the campus, steering them to scenes of disruption caused by the strike. TV shots and newspaper photos depicted classes held in church basements or movie theaters, and long lines at local groceries where students stocked up on potato chips, twinkies, and cans of tuna in lieu of dining hall meals. These stories contradicted the University's claim that business continued "as usual" on the campus. Reports of student discomfort due to the strike also generated protest from parents and alumni, who often were not at all sympathetic to Local 34, but who nonetheless called on the administration to settle fast and return the University to normal.

However, tales of campus disruption were not the only stories turned out by reporters visiting Yale during the strike. The unusual tactics developed by the union or its supporters in the University—such as the "witnesses" or the lawsuit filed by students—were often the focus of a particular story. The unique characteristics of Local 34, and the determination and dignity of the strikers, became the subject of many feature investigations as well.

These reports brought Local 34 more words of encouragement—and more financial support. Tracy Dick, a Yale graduate student who served on Local 34's fundraising committee, believes that fundraising "was just getting off the ground when the strike ended." The committee, she explained, had just begun to contact national sources for contributions—women's groups, international unions, and sympathetic political organizations—when the strikers returned to work.

As any veteran of a long strike realizes, financial difficulties are not the only problems that erode strikers' spirits. Frustration, discouragement, and simple boredom take their toll on the picket lines as well. Local 34's leadership worked hard throughout the strike to combat such feelings, recognizing that preserving strikers' morale was more important than running the strike in a "traditional" fashion. Rather than picket twenty-four hours a day, or attempt to cover the entrances of every building on campus (an essentially impossible task), the union concentrated strikers into fewer picket shifts at selected locations. Individual picket lines were often "collapsed" and drawn together into larger ones in the afternoon to lift strikers' spirits at the end of the day. To lessen the monotony inherent in marching around in a circle, the union regularly sponsored special events or promoted unusual strategies. Marches were held that traversed the University; picket lines were put up around important University functions; students and strikers distributed union literature at the Yale Bowl on game days and evening performances at Yale's Repertory Theatre were picketed and patrons asked to turn in their tickets to show support for the strikers. In fact, many Yale events held during the strike became occasions of a sort for the union as well. When New York mayor Ed Koch refused to move his speech to the Yale Political Union off-campus, he had to be escorted by a police guard through an angry crowd of some 300 union members and supporters shouting "Koch go home!" More people confronted Koch on the picket line than were inside to hear him speak.

Other tactics intended to reinforce the strikers' faith in their cause surfaced as well. In late October, picketers confronted clerical workers who had not gone on strike and asked them to sign a statement indicating that they would turn any salary or benefit increases won for them by the union over to charity, since by working during the strike, scabs were indicating either that they believed the union could not win them anything, or that compensation levels were already adequate. While no such signatures were obtained, this action helped strikers articulate their increasing anger at scabbing C&Ts.

"Speak outs" served similar purposes. Held periodically at different areas of the campus, these events enabled strikers and members of the community to tell their own stories. The speak outs were a rank-and-file forum; union staffers rarely participated. And the union's extensive network of picket captains, joined the union staff in making it a point to keep strikers apprised of displays of support within the Yale community. Their work was supplemented by a good deal of printed material, such as strike bulletins with important announcements, or flyers which explained the University's latest statements and the union's position on them.

These support mechanisms contributed to the lasting power of the strike. By the beginning of November, after five weeks on strike, only 50 to 60 clerical workers had returned to work, and even fewer members of Local 35 had. Yet at this point the University continued to insist that it would never increase its "final offer." The University attempted to make its case directly by deluging students, faculty, alumni, and parents with letters and high-gloss brochures that presented the Yale position. Ads placed in the *Yale Daily News* and in the New Haven papers served the same purpose. President Giamatti granted interviews to the *New York Times* and the *New Haven Register*, neither of which was particularly hard-hitting, however. The *Times*, on whose Board of Directors sat Cyrus Vance, did not grant union spokespeople equal time. For the most part, though, Yale administrators and members of the Corporation avoided direct contact with the press, preferring to eliminate the danger of outside interpretation when making the University's case to the community.

The University also had other, subtler means of getting its point across. In December, the Connecticut Civil Liberties Union (CCLU) held a press conference charging that actions taken by the University during the strike were jeopardizing freedom of expression on the campus. The CCLU cited several instances in which faculty and students supportive of Local 34 had been subjected to pressure and discipline from administration officials and lower level authorities. Some students, for example, were warned by their Residential College masters to remove posters or banners supportive of the union from dormitory walls. Department chairs advised their teaching assistants not to discuss the strike with their students. Yale police told students who attempted to picket on Yale property that such activity was prohibited. Some professional and managerial employees were threatened with unfavorable job evaluations when they spoke with strikers on the picket lines.

In a University setting where one's standing with professors or superiors is of considerable concern to most students and employees, such intimidation could not have been completely ignored. The CCLU warned that there had been "an unwarranted and highly unfortunate chilling of the speech of members of the Yale community." The University did not engage in an across-the-board, well-articulated campaign against pro-union sentiment on the campus, but arbitrary intimidation gravely disturbed the CCLU. Yale University, a supposed bastion of liberal ideals, had been caught engaging in the most illiberal of activities: the suppression of freedom of speech.

To combat Yale's attempt to stifle union support on campus, Local 34 once again took the offensive. It did not simply resist the University's actions, but made a major issue of the fact that such intimidation was taking place. With assistance from a group of supportive students in the Yale Law School, Local 34 collected and publicized information about instances of alleged violations of free speech. Following the CCLU's appearance, the union recalled the report of Yale's own Committee on Freedom of Expression. Posters appeared throughout the campus questioning whether the University still believed, as the report had professed, that "the history of intellectual growth and discovery clearly demonstrates the need for unfettered freedom, the right to think the unthinkable, discuss the unmentionable, and challenge the unchallengeable." The union contrasted Yale's reputation as a haven for intellectual freedom with the activities it engaged in to prevent dissent over its own labor relations policies.

As the strike continued, union leaders remained sensitive to changes in the mood of the Yale community. Many students, faculty, and other union sympathizers continued to walk picket lines with the strikers, yet as the walkout pushed into November, the manifestations of support declined. Students who had once joined the picketers for a while if they had to cross a line to go to class now often left buildings without acknowledging the strikers' presence. Faculty members who had avoided picking up mail or using their offices began to walk through picket lines without apology. Many Local 34 members came to believe that the University community—even their supporters—had adjusted to the disruption caused by the strike and was no longer disturbed by the sight of picket lines. Some strikers complained that they had started to feel "invisible" after the first show of support subsided. Union members and the Local 34 leadership searched for ways to shake the Yale community out of this acceptance of the strike's "routine." When some students on one of the union support committees proposed a "moratorium" on all Yale activities, Local 34 quickly endorsed the idea.

A moratorium had been considered by many people early in the strike. The proposal was to ask for a boycott of all Yale activities, including social events and classes (even those taught off-campus), to show support for the union. The impetus for such an action seemed even greater by November when both strikers and their supporters needed to reinforce their commitment. Mobilizing for a moratorium, it was believed, would give strikers an opportunity to remind already sympathetic students and faculty that being supportive to the union meant more than simply wearing a button. Moreover, by raising the need for such a boycott with other members of the Yale community, Local 34 members hoped to generate more support for the union. After some discussion within both the union and the support groups, the moratorium was set for November 14-16, Wednesday through Friday, preceding Yale's week-long Thanksgiving break.

Even Local 34's leadership did not fully anticipate the impact that organizing for the moratorium would have on the campus. Members of the Yale community who had managed to adjust to the picket lines were confronted anew by the strike, as union members urged them to observe the moratorium. For some two weeks, New Haven's sidewalks, the strike headquarters, and nearby restaurants were crowded with moratorium proponents aggressively pressing their case with faculty members, students, and management and professional employees. The union held "town meetings" in different areas of the campus and encouraged all members of the community to attend to discuss the upcoming action. They drew large audiences, as did a meeting called by graduate student supporters for all Yale's graduate and professional students. Discussions about the moratorium frequently grew angry as clerical and technical workers who might once have politely asked for help from people they had worked years for now demanded this support. For some Local 34 members, the moratorium represented the first time that they had directly confronted professors, doctors, or administrators about the strike. Many student supporters likewise played an active role, often engaging in angry arguments with their professors or their friends, pushing them to cancel or boycott classes.

Some of the stiffest resistance to the moratorium came from heretofore supportive students and faculty. Many argued that the union was asking too much of them—that they had an inviolable obligation to teach or to study and that they had done as much as they could by attending rallies or moving classes off campus. Some professors, particularly junior faculty members, believed that showing support for the moratorium was too great a risk, for the University made it clear that canceling classes during this period would be "unacceptable." The Deans of Yale College and of the Graduate School sent a memo to the faculty stating that professors and graduate assistants "must continue to meet their teaching responsibilities during this difficult period." In some departments, the warnings were more direct: the chair of the Philosophy Department, for example, issued a memo indicating that faculty members who observe the moratorium "should expect a loss of pay and may be subject to other penalties." The CCLU criticized the implicit threats which characterized the University's response to the moratorium, because "persons who chose to view participation in the moratorium as an act of personal conscience were not fully informed of the consequences of the intended act." Such vagueness served the University's purposes, and many graduate students and untenured junior faculty members came to believe that support for the moratorium would put them in jeopardy.

Union members and student advocates of the moratorium attempted to overcome both the principled objections to the moratorium and the fear of reprisals voiced by faculty members and students. Clerical workers pointed out the risks and the hardship that they and the members of Local 35 were enduring through the strike, and they asked that sympathetic professors and students help share their burden. Deborah Chernoff, one of Local 34's most active rank-and-file leaders, recalls her discussions with friendly faculty members. "If you are truly supportive," she urged them, "support means occasionally putting your own comfort on the line, whether comfort means being respected by the chairman in your department, or whether you're up for tenure and you're afraid that 'disloyalty' to the institution will jeopardize your tenure; if you're really supportive of an issue and you think it's critical, you're willing to take those kinds of risks.''

Strikers pointed out that a three-day cessation of activities would cause only minor hardship for students, and that in many areas of the campus classes were frequently canceled for less pressing reasons. Local 34 members recognized faculty members' commitment to their students, but argued that the obligation to teach should not necessarily overshadow all other moral responsibilities. Many supporters of the action also believed that a successful moratorium might force the University to negotiate and settle the dispute, something that would be far more beneficial to students than allowing the strike to drag on.

Surprises of two sorts greeted the moratorium. Sympathetic professors who failed to cancel classes were balanced by faculty members and students who had not previously identified themselves as union supporters who now honored the moratorium. The entire computer science department faculty, for example, observed the moratorium, with the exception of the chair. There was no sure way to gauge the precise effect of the moratorium: how many classes were canceled or rescheduled, how many employees called in sick or took vacation days, how many people who had been using the library or the gym stayed away for three days. Yet the union counted the moratorium a tremendous success not only because some areas of the campus resembled a ghost town but also because the impact that it had both on union members and on the Yale community in general.

The three days of the moratorium boosted morale. Far from a period of inactivity, the moratorium featured almost continuous events organized by the union, students, and faculty. Benefitted by unseasonably warm and sunny weather, the union led marches through the campus and held speak outs drawing overflow crowds; professors, graduate students, and union members gave talks on comparable worth, labor history, and feminism; Sergei Eisenstein's *The Strike* and Charlie Chaplin's *Modern Times* were screened at strike headquarters. Large picket lines formed early in the morning at key areas on campus and strikers walked with friends from different areas of the University. On Thursday, strikers and supporters marched through the Science area of campus for a tour of Yale's wealth, during which the University's huge investments and corporate connections were detailed to the crowd. The moratorium climaxed Friday morning with a rally at the medical school where some 40 professors from New York City universities arrived to show their support.

That the moratorium severely taxed the Yale community in many respects was beneficial to Local 34. The atmosphere of challenge and confrontation eroded the much esteemed "collegiality" of the University. As strikers became more openly hostile to scabs, as students entered into heated debate with their professors, as classmates engaged in shouting matches on street corners, even those who had done their best to remain aloof had trouble ignoring the disintegration of Yale's community due to the strike. The Yale administration's insistence that business at the University was continuing "as usual" rang even more hollow after the moratorium. More and more people, many of whom had kept silent before the moratorium, began to insist that an end to the strike was essential to the University's well-being.

While urging people to observe the moratorium, many strikers made it clear to students and faculty members that they would no longer regard friendly chats on the picket lines as sufficient to ensure the clerical workers' gratitude. For many liberal professors and students who had not observed the moratorium, the hostility encountered from moratorium advocates proved enormously upsetting. They looked for other ways to demonstrate their allegiance to the workers, and many who had done little before began to appear at rallies, to sign petitions, or to write letters to Yale administrators urging negotiations.

Union insiders suspected that one of the more important documents produced about the strike came as a result of moratorium pressure. Shortly after the moratorium ended, three professors from the Yale Law School, who despite the repeated urgings of strikers and many of their students, had not canceled their classes, nonetheless were convinced that "as faculty members [they] had a responsibility to make some assessment of the impact of the strike upon the educational and research mission of the University." Owen Fiss, Joseph Goldstein, and Burke Marshall issued a report in December which provided a damning evaluation of life at Yale during the strike. "We turn to you now," they wrote in their cover letter addressed to the Yale faculty, "because our common cause was severely damaged during the strike, because our individual efforts were insufficient to safeguard adequately that cause, and because further interruption of our work, the work of our students, and the work of our staff—the University's work—can be neither justified nor tolerated." They found that the strike was having a detrimental effect on almost all aspects of University life, from the libraries and laboratories to social activities and intellectual conversation. Its authors had intended the report to be used only by fellow faculty members, who were asked to urge the administration to submit outstanding issues to a third party for settlement. However, Local 34 leaders had it printed in pamphlet form and sent it to the parents of all Yale undergraduates, who had already received a number of letters from the Yale administration assuring them that their children's lives on the campus remained essentially unaffected by the strike. The union also placed a full-page ad in *The Chronicle of Higher Education* quoting from the report.

The University's November 12 call for a resumption of negotiations probably resulted from the moratorium build-up. Union leaders hoped that the momentum from the planned moratorium might force the administration to make serious concessions, but in the end they were disappointed. On Thursday evening, Local 34 negotiators walked away from the table in disgust when it became clear that the University would not increase the dollar amount of its proposal. The administration's recalcitrance came in the face of a significant compromise offered by the union, which according to the University's own calculations, reduced Local 34's salary and benefit demands from 40 to 30 million dollars. Union members, embittered by the administration's calling of the union back into negotiations with nothing new to offer, entered into the final day of moratorium activities in an angry and determined mood. Picket lines that Friday were particularly large and loud. At the conclusion of the moratorium Friday afternoon, union members looked towards the Thanksgiving holiday with their spirits bolstered and their animosity towards the University administration heightened. By this time the members of Local 34 and Local 35 had been walking picket lines for seven weeks.

Reinforcing the strikers' determination, as it turned out, was particularly important at this time, for the union was about to introduce another controversial proposal. The idea was first discussed as a possible response should Local 35 lose the arbitration initiated by the University, and thus be ordered by the courts to cross Local 34's picket lines and return to work.

While anticipating the arbitrator's decision, some union members suggested that if the ruling went against Local 35, it might be best if both Local 34 and Local 35 went back to work together, even if the white collar workers had not yet reached a settlement. The two locals could then await the expiration of Local 35's contract on January 19, 1985, and if necessary return to the picket lines to strike together, without the threat of court interference. Such a strategy was made possible by the partial contract enacted the previous April, which provided Local 34 members the protection of a grievance procedure if they should return to work with salary and benefit issues outstanding. Since the blue collar workers in Local 35 were honoring their sister local's picket lines and were not technically on strike themselves, they could of course return to their jobs under the protection of their old contract.

When, at the outset of the strike, the University had initiated the legal challenge to Local 35's right to observe the C&Ts' picket lines, the unions anticipated a ruling within a few weeks. However, by mid-November, the judge hearing the case had not yet announced a decision. Some union members, considering the back-to-work idea, proposed at staff meetings that even if the union *won* the case, it might be smart if both locals returned to work until January 19 anyway. Thus the "Home for the Holidays" or "Striking on the Inside" program was first suggested. Its advocates argued that there were several reasons why the back-to-work plan made sense. First, many

Local 35 leaders endorsed it because by mid-November, they did not feel in a particularly good position to enter into their own up-coming negotiations with the University. Because their members were observing clerical workers' picket lines and were thus not at their jobs, it was difficult for the Local 35 leadership to go through the normal process of getting in touch with the membership and for-mulating their own demands to present to the University. Many Local 34 members believed that they owed it to Local 35 to do what they could to help make it possible for the service and maintenance workers to have some time to develop their proposals.

But there were direct advantages for Local 34 as well in the Home for the Holidays plan. By Thanksgiving, many Local 34 members were looking towards the upcoming Christmas holiday with anxie-ty. The campus would be virtually shut down from mid-December to mid-January, and the balmy autumn weather the strikers had enjoyed thus far would not last forever. Rather than picket empty buildings in cold and snowy weather, advocates of Home for the Holidays argued, it would be best to return to work for a while and collect a few weeks of pay—which would make the holidays easier for union members and allow them to pay some pressing bills. Moreover, during the University's Christmas break, the return to work would allow strikers to take advantage of five paid vacation days. The University could not legally prevent Local 34 members from returning to work, except through a lockout. If the University would have taken such a drastic step, scabs along with union members would have been prevented from entering buildings, and Yale would have been required to pay unemployment compensation to locked-out workers. In addition, the administration undoubtedly recognized that locking out employees could only further damage the Univer-sity's reputation. Yale took no official action to block the strikers' return.

It was in this return to work that many of the union's leaders saw the greatest possibilities for the Home for the Holidays plan. They referred to it as "taking the strike inside," and like the Industrial Workers of the World which in the early twentieth century had advocated striking on the job, they believed it to be more of an offensive than a defensive program. Being inside, they argued, would give strikers access to many people that they had been cut off from for weeks. Union members would be able to talk with scabs and strikebreakers, and confront them about their actions. In particular, Local 34 members wanted to get in touch with the C&Ts who had initially joined the strike but had since returned to their jobs. If these workers could be convinced that Local 34 could win, they might walk out with the union again, if it became necessary, in January. Home for the Holidays would bring strikers in contact with many other groups that the union was also anxious to reach: faculty members, doctors, management and professional employees. As with the moratorium earlier, many union members saw the return to work as the perfect opportunity to force those who preferred to ignore the strike to face up to it. For union supporters, too, Home for the Holidays presented new possibilities: students who had been strictly honoring picket lines could enter campus buildings and explain the union's position to other students and faculty.

Home for the Holidays was intensely debated among the rank-and-file staff for two weeks before finally being endorsed and introduced to all on the picket lines in late November. Many members were vehemently opposed to the proposal when they first heard it. Kim McLaughlin, one of the union's paid organizers, remembered the reaction at the medical school:

The first day [Home for the Holidays] hit the streets, all the picket lines in the medical area went into a major revolt . . . . I thought we were all about to get strung up by our toes . . . . People's feelings after eight weeks on strike were "Are we winning or are we losing?" and suddenly you drop a plan like going back to work on them and their instant reaction is "We're losing. Oh, my God, we're losing, and they just don't think we can take it if they tell us."

Most of the opposition to the Home for the Holidays plan reflected the view that it was not a winning strategy. People were afraid that returning to work without a settlement would look like defeat to the media and to the rest of the Yale community. In fact, many members believed that it *would* be a defeat, for they would be returning to their offices and laboratories without the contract they had joined the picket lines to obtain. The disruption caused by the strike—the backlogged correspondence, delayed research, and mishandled billings and payrolls—would be undone if strikers returned to their jobs, and with Local 35 members back as well, food service and building maintenance would also be restored. Although most of the campus is quiet during the holidays, in a few areas, such as undergraduate admissions and the bursar's office, the first weeks of the new year are hectic periods. Strikers in such offices who had anticipated upcoming chaos due to their absence were reluctant to go back in and prevent it. In addition, many union members, despite the combativeness of the rank-and-file leadership, were not anxious to return to their offices and laboratories to face the hostility of unfriendly faculty members and administrators and the antipathy of scabs. Some strikers flatly stated that if they had to go back to work without a contract, they would not come out again if the strike commenced on January 19, and Local 34 members who opposed Home for the Holidays believed that such feelings were widespread. The Local 35 members who were not enthusiastic about the plan had a similar fear: that if the blue-collar workers had to strike on January 19, many clerical and technical workers would not come back out to honor *their* picket lines.

The debate within the union over the Home for the Holidays proposal was as intense as any had been since the struggle over the partial contract in April. "For days," Kim McLaughlin remembers, "twenty hours in a row, it was fight after fight after fight." Yet many participants viewed such discussion in a positive light. Warren Heyman, one of the union's paid staff members, recalls his reaction to the Home for the Holidays controversy: "I thought it was an amazing experience. It was democracy in action. People were debating, people were discussing; yes, there were even some yelling and screaming and crying—but it would be great if we could have that kind of discussion before a presidential election."

What might be most noteworthy about the Home for the Holidays proposal is that it was introduced in the first place. Because labor leaders often believe that controversy within a union undermines solidarity (and might also threaten the leadership's position), it is not commonplace to introduce innovative tactics into the midst of a bitter strike. That Local 34's leaders did so indicates both their faith in the rank and file and their belief that debate, even in times of crisis, builds a union's strength. Although Home for the Holidays and the partial contract were both controversial programs, the debates surrounding them differed in one important respect. Because Local 34's members had a good deal of time to consider the Home for the Holidays proposal before voting on it, the discussion about returning to work did not threaten the union's cohesiveness. Although some members opposed to the Home for the Holidays expressed resentment towards the union leadership at the outset of the debate, little such feeling existed by the time of the vote on the plan. By then few strikers could be found saying that they themselves would not return to the picket lines if it became necessary—though many union members remained fearful that "other workers" would not rejoin the strike. While the partial contract was adopted largely due to the rank and file's trust in the Local 34 Negotiating Committee and union staff, the Home for the Holidays vote reflected some two and a half weeks of thorough discussion of the viability of the strategy.

On November 29, Local 34 strikers voted 800-250 to take down the picket lines and return to work on December 4, with the added proviso that if *either* Local 34's or Local 35's contract was not settled on January 19, both locals would return to the streets. In addition, the Local 34 membership reaffirmed its resolve and voted once again to reject Yale's "final offer" by a 952-79 margin, an extraordinary tally after ten weeks of the strike. This vote also demolished the notion suggested by Local 34's detractors that the Home for the Holidays debate had undermined allegiance to the union and commitment to the strike. On the morning of December 4, strikers gathered in coffee shops or in front of Yale buildings. Excited and apprehensive, they sang union songs or chatted nervously about the day to come. Then, together, as they had walked the picket lines for the last ten weeks, they marched into their offices and their laboratories, ready to begin striking on the inside.

Sooner or Later, You'll Win

When the striking members of Local 34 finally did enter Yale's office and laboratory buildings to return to work, none of them really knew what to expect. In some offices, supervisors attempted immediately to reestablish their authority over workers who had discovered a new sense of freedom and self-respect on the picket lines the preceding ten weeks. In other areas, workers were welcomed back to work as if the strike had never occurred. And in some parts of Yale, supervisors and faculty members, many of whom had done little or nothing to support their striking support staff, went to elaborate and self-consciously gracious measures to welcome the C&Ts back.

The union began to refer to the contrasting atmospheres as the "war zones" and the "bore zones." The "war zones," typified by Sterling Library and the medical school, represented those work environments where management had always been most hostile to union organizing. Upon their return, strikers in these areas found that little had changed. In the Library, for instance, supervisors informed union members that only those employees who had continued to work during the strike would remain eligible for "flex time," a University policy under which employees in certain departments could set their own hours as long as they worked a specified number of hours per week. Library management also imposed a new rule barring C&Ts who worked in other buildings from the Library cafeteria; known as the "Sterling Spoon," this cafeteria had long served as a gathering place for union members from throughout Yale's library system. For returning strikers, these new rules seemed designed to punish and discourage union activity, to drive home who was boss at Yale.

In the "bore zones," the reception was less vindictive and management acted as if all had been satisfactorily resolved. Here the methods used to reestablish hierarchical working relationships were often more subtle. In some offices, for example, supervisors presented their returning clerical staff with flowers. While some found this gesture gratifying, others thought that it was condescending. In other departments, much to the returning striker's disgust, supervisors tried to avoid confronting the implications of the strike by simply pretending that it had never taken place. As Suzy Voigt recalls of that first day back, "In one area where all four secretaries were out on strike, when they came back in, the doctors didn't exactly know what to do, and one of them finally went up to his secretary and said, 'I was going to bring flowers, but then I didn't—I thought maybe it would be better to make believe nothing had happened.' Well, he couldn't have said anything worse. This young woman said, 'You were going to make believe nothing had happened? What do you think I've been doing for the last ten weeks?' It was as if there wasn't anything they could say which would strike the right note, since none of these people had done anything to back us up during the strike."

One way in which supervisors tried to ignore the fact that there had been a strike was to try to refuse to discuss the issues still in dispute. But Home for the Holidays had not been conceived by Local 34's leadership as simply a defensive plan whereby the strikers could get out of the cold weather for six weeks. The leadership therefore pushed all the members to continue to talk to their supervisors about the strike. Union members reminded all those who were trying to ignore the dispute that the return to work was only temporary—the strike would resume on January 19 if the University had not settled with both Local 34 and Local 35 by that time. Many C&Ts began wearing a button which simply asked, "Is it January 19th yet?" Others posted homemade calendars in their offices, whose final date was the 19th of January, and began to cross off each day that passed without a settlement being reached. Student support groups also tried to remind students and faculty alike that if they did not speak out before the semester ended, when they returned from Christmas break they were likely to find their lives disrupted once again.

Despite these efforts, as the final days of the fall semester came and went, many of the C&Ts, and most of the students and faculty, were less interested in arguing about the strike than in anticipating a much-needed period of relaxation during the holiday season. Virtually everyone at Yale looked forward to a break from the almost incessant stress which had accompanied the strike, and many postponed even thinking about the possibility of another strike until after the New Year. Perhaps as a result, no further progress had been made in negotiations by the time Christmas break finally settled over the campus.

While many of the C&Ts were too drained by the strike and the readjustment to work to continue agitating over the outstanding issues, the union itself organized several actions designed to keep pressure on the administration. Five days after the return to the offices and labs, Local 34 held a demonstration, timed to coincide with that weekend's December meeting of the Yale Corporation. The rally attracted almost 1,000 students, faculty, C&Ts, Local 35 members, New Haven residents, and trade unionists from all over the northeast, including delegations of clerical workers from Harvard, Princeton, Columbia, and Rutgers. Local 34's alumni supporters released to the press letters and petitions they had sent to President Giamatti urging the University to settle with the two unions.

Still, as students and faculty began to trickle back to the campus for the spring semester, little progress had been made in negotiations between the University and the unions. As the second semester opened on January 14 with only five days remaining before the strike deadline, no settlement had been reached with either Local 34 or Local 35.

By the middle of the week, it began to appear that there might be hope after all. Three days before the strike deadline, Local 34 and Local 35 held a campus-wide rally to show the administration that the unions were still determined to walk out together if both contracts had not been settled. That night, both the University and Local 34 agreed on a dental plan for the C&Ts. The next night, agreement was reached on improvements in Yale's pension plan for the white collar workers. But while progress was being made on the Local

34 contract, there was no time to conduct negotiations with Local 35. Optimistic that agreements for both unions could be reached with a little more time, both unions therefore agreed to push back the strike deadline a week, to January 26. Finally, in an all-night session, negotiators for Local 34 and for Yale hammered out the final provisions on salary increases, job security, and the other outstanding issues. At approximately 5:00 on the morning of January 19—the original strike deadline—an exhausted but jubilant Local 34 Negotiating Committee—after 91 negotiating sessions, left the Hall of Graduate Studies with a draft of the young union's first contract.

The contract was overwhelmingly ratified the following week. The agreement included a 20.25% across-the-board salary increase over three years retroactive to July 1, 1984, and provided for the systems of "Steps" and "Slotting" that Local 34 had sought. The union also won better pensions, a dental plan, and improved job security. The contract called for creation of a joint union-management "Job Description and Classification Committee" to hear appeals from employees who felt that they were being paid too little because their jobs were not fairly classified. This committee was also authorized to investigate whether the University's overall job classification needed revamping. Wilhelm pronounced the settlement "an outstanding first contract."

Local 34's settlement left most of Yale's unionized employees, as well as most students and faculty, optimistic that the administration would settle with the blue collar workers and avoid another strike. The University's negotiators for the Local 35 contract were still talking tough, but most observers agreed that the Yale Corporation had in fact decided over the Christmas break that Yale could not afford another walkout.

While Local 35's contract proposals included wage hikes, pension improvements, and a comprehensive dental plan, the issue most important to the union's members was that of job security. The union wanted the new contract to include more stringent prohibitions against the University's practice of subcontracting out work which could be done by Local 35 members, protections against layoffs, and a guarantee of twelve months of employment for those workers whose regular jobs were geared to providing services to Yale's students, most of whom are at the University for only nine months of the year.

When negotiations began on Monday, January 22, Local 35's negotiating team was confident that by week's end, they too would have a new, and satisfactory, contract. But no issues were settled on Monday, or on Tuesday, and tension began to return to the University's campus, as people started once again to ask each other the familiar question, "What's happening in negotiations?" It appeared that the answer was once again, "Nothing."

However, the leaders of Local 35 and Local 34 continued to remind their members that "negotiations take place in the offices and labs of the University, and not in the negotiating room." They believed that the administration would be willing to make significant concessions on the issues of concern to the blue-collar workers only if union members and their supporters demonstrated to the administration that they were willing to stand up to the University and walk out over Local 35's contract just as they had done for Local 34's.

The unions and their supporters among the students and faculty decided to take actions to convince the administration that they considered the Local 35 contract to be as important as Local 34's. Perhaps foremost among these was the circulation of a petition among Local 34's members in which the clericals and technicals pledged to honor Local 35's picket lines in case of a strike; during the week, a large group of Local 34 members triumphantly walked in on negotiations to deliver these petitions—bearing more than a thousand signatures—to the administration's negotiating team. The unions also organized a demonstration that week replete with signs that read, for example, "You did it for us, Local 35, Now we'll do it for you," and that bore other messages not lost on the administration. Students staged their own rally, joined by members of Local 35, at a subcontracting site on campus to dramatize the importance of the job security issue and to show that students would support the blue collar union. And on the eve of the strike deadline, students and Local 34 members gathered in the corridor outside the negotiating room to pressure Yale's team—which was forced to "run the gauntlet" each time it entered or left negotiations. Finally, in the early morning hours of January 26, a tight-lipped University negotiating committee filed out of the negotiating room, followed by a grinning Local 35 team, which announced that a settlement of all outstanding issues had been reached.

Afterword

In a period that has seen few union victories, the achievements of Local 34 at Yale gave the labor movement something to cheer about. Local 34's success came about not through flashy schemes or gimmicks—no jackets were given away, no credit cards were offered. Instead, Local 34 relied largely on the same tactics that had brought the now moribund unions of the AFL-CIO their great victories earlier in this century. Many of today's union leaders would do well to examine not only Local 34's example, but their own organizations' histories, to determine how to turn the labor movement around. Like the CIO organizing drives of the 1930s, Local 34 promoted a high level of rank-and-file participation, during both the initial organizing campaign and the fight for a first contract. Union organizers stressed that the local's strength would come not through the size of the International's treasury, but through the conviction and involvement of the C&Ts themselves. Local 34's campaign became a moral struggle, as the C&Ts demanded not only much deserved wage increases but also recognition and respect. Facing a powerful and hostile management, Local 34 responded with innovative strategies that continually kept the Yale administration off-guard and reinvigorated the union's membership. Local 34's approach to organizing was once basic to the labor movement. Too often today, union officials, many of whom would be threatened by an active rank-and-file, emphasize the services unions provide rather than the collective strength they make possible.

Much as some of Local 34's tactics resemble those of organizing drives of the past, in other respects the Yale campaign represents an important new phenomenon in labor history. By making pay equity a major theme of its campaign, Local 34 demonstrated that unions can make "women's issues" fighting principles—and win. If unions are to become attractive to the unorganized majority of the American workforce, which is increasingly female, then women's concerns must be a central focus in new organizing drives. The members of Local 34 made it clear that women are fully capable of building and leading strong unions. Whether other labor leaders, still mostly male, realize this remains to be seen.

Local 34's story is, of course, not yet concluded. Many questions raised by the union's initial success must wait for answers. It will be important to note, for example, how Local 34 endeavors to maintain its strength over the next several years. Promoting rank-and-file involvement during contract negotiations and strikes is one thing; maintaining such enthusiasm during less dramatic periods is a more difficult task. As with many clerical bargaining units, Local 34 faces an additional problem which could serve to undermine union strength: turnover. It is estimated that at least one-third of the women and men who went through the 1984 strike will no longer work as Yale C&Ts by the time the next negotiating sessions begin. Local 34 thus faces the loss of many of its experienced members and rank-and-file leaders.

Shortly after the Yale strike, C&Ts at Columbia University, members of UAW District 65, won a contract as well. District 65 organizers acknowledged the major impact the Yale drive had had on workers at Columbia. What is less clear is what effect, in fact what application, Local 34's success will have for clerical workers outside a university setting. Universities have one weakness that few other industries share: they cannot move. Other major employers of clerical workers—banks and insurance agencies, for example— might consider transferring their major operations if threatened by an organizing drive in one city (something computer technology makes eminently possible). Such industries, in addition, are less likely to be as immediately hurt, though they are vulnerable, to the type of corporate campaign utilized by Local 34. An "enlightened" image is less vital to a bank than it is to a university like Yale. Clerical organizers in private industry may find that local campaigns are not enough.

It is also too early to tell what impact Local 34's victory will have on the New Haven community outside Yale. While the union appealed to various community leaders for support throughout the strike, Yale's dominant position in the city of New Haven—and the contrast between the University's wealth and the city's poverty—was not made a major issue. Local 34's leaders undoubtedly recognized that Yale is more concerned with complaints from faculty, alumni, students and their parents than it is with the criticisms of New Haven citizens. Yet, by focusing on the Yale community rather than the New Haven community during the strike, the union missed an opportunity to become a major force in New Haven politics. Local 34 may yet choose to do so—perhaps when its position at Yale becomes more secure. But the possibility exists that unions within universities can become as insular as the institutions in which they organize.

Because of generally uninspired top union leadership, most of today's labor *movement* is happening on the local level. However, it is not a foregone conclusion that these local struggles will greatly affect the outlook and policies of the AFL-CIO's international unions. Local union leaders who initiate aggressive or innovative tactics have often encountered stern disapproval, and in some cases concerted opposition, from their international officers. In contrast, the Hotel and Restaurant Employee's Union, Local 34's parent organization, provided full organizational and financial support for the Yale strike. HERE has also scored other victories in the past several years, in Boston and Las Vegas, for example. It is not clear how much these campaigns have transformed this enormously wealthy international, not previously renowned for its rank-and-file involvement. Whether Local 34's dynamic and democratic orientation will be promoted throughout the Hotel and Restaurant Workers and the AFL-CIO, or merely tolerated by the labor establishment, is as yet an open question. But the clerical workers' victory at Yale, along with many other local struggles throughout the country, may signal the beginning of a revitalized labor movement. If so, the thrust forward will come from the movement's greatest source of strength—the union members themselves.

Update 1995

Many changes have taken place at Yale since this book was written. The university's administration has seen much upheaval: A. Bartlett Giamatti stepped down as Yale's president in 1986 and became commissioner of Major League Baseball shortly thereafter; Giamatti died in 1987. Benno Schmidt succeeded Giamatti as president of Yale but left six years later after a rocky tenure as the university's chief administrator. Yale's current president, Richard Levin, a former professor in the university's economics department, took office in the fall of 1993. Many of the other administrators who played key roles in the 1984 strike have since left Yale, and the Board of Trustees has also undergone revision.

Much is now different about Local 34 as well. Since its 1985 victory, Local 34 has twice bargained for contracts with Yale, both of which were achieved without a strike. The agreements brought the membership new and innovative benefits. In 1988 the union won the revamped job description system Local 34 had long insisted was critical if clerical and technical workers were to achieve pay equity. New contract language secured in 1992 addressed the looming problem of layoffs: any Local 34 member with as little as a year's seniority, if let go by Yale, will receive six months' salary and benefits from the university (workers with six or more years' seniority are given a full year's compensation). Such security, especially important in the midst of a recession, will no doubt help stabilize Local 34's membership in the years to come. The blue-collar workers in Local 35, whose contract now expires when Local 34's does, also won greater protection against subcontracting in their 1992 agreement.

But contract language is not all that is new for the unions at Yale.

Locals 34 and 35, whose combined membership figures are approximately equal to what they were in 1984, have determined to see union protection extended to another workforce at Yale: the graduate students who serve as research and teaching assistants at the university. The Graduate Employees Student Organization (GESO) is currently organizing in an effort to secure formal recognition from the administration, and GESO's campaign has been fiercely supported by the blue- and white-collar unions already in place at Yale. If the graduate students are successful in their push for recognition, theirs will be the first organization of its kind in the Ivy League, and union power at Yale will be further strengthened.

Despite these new directions, for Local 34 some things remain unchanged. Though the union has not needed, since 1985, to resort to a strike to win additional contract clauses, Local 34 has not modified its belief that organizing should not cease when an agreement is signed. Creative strategies remain hallmarks of the unions at Yale. Locals 34 and 35 have staged one-day and three-hour strikes to demonstrate support for the graduate students' organization; these actions disrupted campus life and garnered publicity for GESO, which was of course precisely the point. During the 1992 contract negotiations, as Benno Schmidt threatened to cut departments and eliminate countless clerical and technical positions, Local 34 produced a video entitled "Am I Blue?" that documented the ways in which the university would be hurt by such cutbacks. As had been done during the 1984 strike with the report issued by Law School faculty, Local 34 distributed "Am I Blue?" to a wide audience— including students' parents, Yale alumni, and guidance counselors at selected high schools. Such high-profile and high-pressure tactics continue to be central to Local 34's repertoire and no doubt play a large part in the union's further successes.

A decade after the clerical and technical workers first walked out at Yale University, the labor movement in this country, generally speaking, remains weak. But the plans that could be used to reconstruct and reinvigorate American unions are not hard to find. Local 34's initial victory—and now its increasing strength—continue to provide an excellent blueprint.